PENNINE BRIDLEWAY

Derbyshire to the
South Pennines

PENNINE BRIDLEWAY

Derbyshire to the
South Pennines

Sue Viccars

Photographs by Mike Williams

AURUM PRESS

The
Countryside
Agency

Acknowledgements

I would like to thank Julie Thompson from the Countryside Agency in Manchester; Jenny Southwell for sorting out all kinds of strange queries; Mike Williams for his superb photography, as well as large amounts of practical and moral support; Jon Sparks for off-road cycling tips; all those people I met along the way – especially in TICs – who willingly supplied me with information; and Piers Burnett of Aurum Press for giving me the chance to go exploring!

Dedication
This book is dedicated to the memory of Lady Mary Towneley

First published in 2004 by Aurum Press Ltd
in association with the Countryside Agency

Text copyright © 2004 Sue Viccars
Photographs © 2004 Countryside Agency

◙ Ordnance Survey® This product includes mapping data licensed from Ordnance Survey® with the permission of the Controller of Her Majesty's Stationery Office. © Crown copyright 2004. All rights reserved. Licence number 43453U.

Ordnance Survey and Travelmaster are registered trademarks and the Ordnance Survey symbol and Explorer are trademarks of Ordnance Survey, the national mapping agency of Great Britain.

A catalogue record for this book is available from the British Library.

ISBN 1 85410 957 X

1 3 5 7 9 10 8 6 4 2
2005 2007 2008 2006 2004

Book design by Robert Updegraff
Printed and bound in Italy by Printer Trento Srl

Cover photograph: *Stoodley Pike monument from below Blackshaw Head.*
Title-page photograph: *View over Hayfield from the summit of Lantern Pike.*

CONTENTS

HOW TO USE THIS GUIDE

This guide to the 117-mile (188-kilometre) southern section of the Pennine Bridleway National Trail is in three parts:

• The introduction, which provides historical background on the area and advice for walkers, horse-riders and cyclists.

• The trail itself, split into eight chapters, with maps opposite the description for each route section. Alternative starting points are given for cyclists (Middleton Top) and horse-riders (Hartington), and separate routes for the three groups of user described for the Hayfield to Uppermill section. The distances noted at the head of each chapter represent the total length of the route in that section. Information is also given on places of interest passed through, or which can be seen from the route. Key sites are numbered both in the text and on the maps to make it easier to follow the route description.

• The last part supplies useful information, such as local transport links, accommodation and organisations.

The maps have been prepared by the Ordnance Survey® using 1:25 000 Explorer® maps as a base. The line of the Pennine Bridleway is shown highlighted in yellow, with the status of each section – byway or bridleway, for example – shown in green underneath (see key on inside front cover). These rights-of-way markings also indicate the precise alignment of the Pennine Bridleway, which you should follow on the ground. In some cases the yellow line on these maps may indicate a different route to that shown on older maps; you are recommended to follow the yellow route in this guide, which will be waymarked with the distinctive acorn symbol ♣ used for all National Trails. Any parts of the Pennine Bridleway that might be difficult to follow on the ground are clearly highlighted in the route description, and important points to watch out for are marked with letters in each chapter, both in the text and on the maps. *Some maps start on a right-hand page and continue on the left-hand page – black arrows (➤) at the edge of the maps indicate the start point.*

Should there be a need to divert the Pennine Bridleway from the route shown in this guide, to allow maintenance work to take place or because the route has had to be changed, you are advised to follow any waymarks or signs along the trail.

Distance Checklist

approx. distance from previous location

location	miles	km
Middleton Top (*start for cyclists/walkers*)	0	0
Minninglow (Gotham / Pike Hall)	6.6	10.6
Parsley Hay	4.9	7.9
Hartington (*start for horse-riders/walkers*)	0	0
Parsley Hay	1.8	2.9
Pomeroy	3.9	6.3
Chelmorton	1.4	2.3
Wormhill	5.1	8.2
Peak Forest	5.6	9.0
Rushop Edge (A625)	2.8	4.5
Hayfield – *horse-riders currently stop here*	5.8	9.3
CYCLISTS' ROUTE		
Charlesworth – *from Hayfield*	7.4	11.9
Lees Hill	6.4	10.3
WALKERS' ROUTE		
Hollingworth – *from Hayfield*	10.1	16.3
Lees Hill	2.1	3.4
HORSE-RIDERS' ROUTE – *resuming at Torside on the Longendale Trail*		
(Torside to Tintwistle link for riders)	(3.5)	(5.6)
Lees Hill – *from Tintwhistle*	2.0	3.2
Carrbrook – *from Lees Hill*	3.2	5.1
Greenfield	2.3	3.7
Uppermill	1.1	1.8
Diggle	1.9	3.1
Hollingworth Lake Visitor Centre (near Littleborough)	10.6	17.1
Summit	4.6	7.4
Broadley	7.3	11.7
Waterfoot	7.4	11.9
Lumb	2.4	3.9
Holme Chapel	5.2	8.4
Blackshaw Head (near Hebden Bridge)	13.0	20.9
Mankinholes	6.1	9.8
Bottomley (Walsden)	3.1	5.0
Summit	1.5	2.4

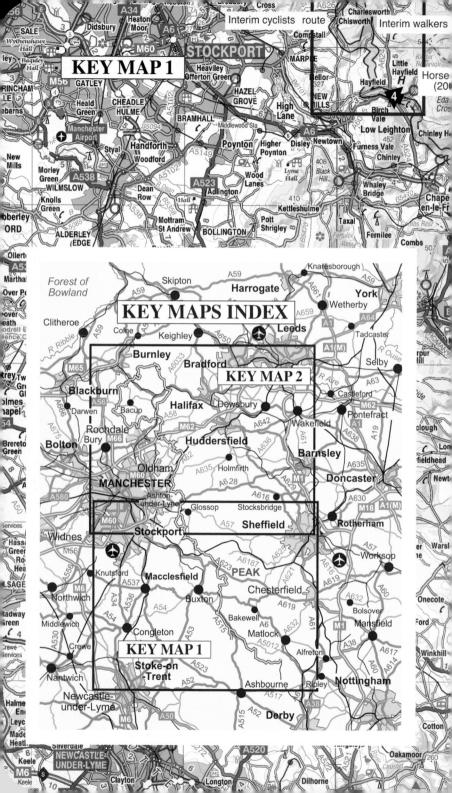

KEY MAPS

—— Pennine Bridleway

▲**1** Chapter start point

0 km   5

0 miles   5

Based on Ordnance Survey Road Map

currently here

Hartington
start for horse-riders/walkers

Middleton Top
start for cyclists/walkers

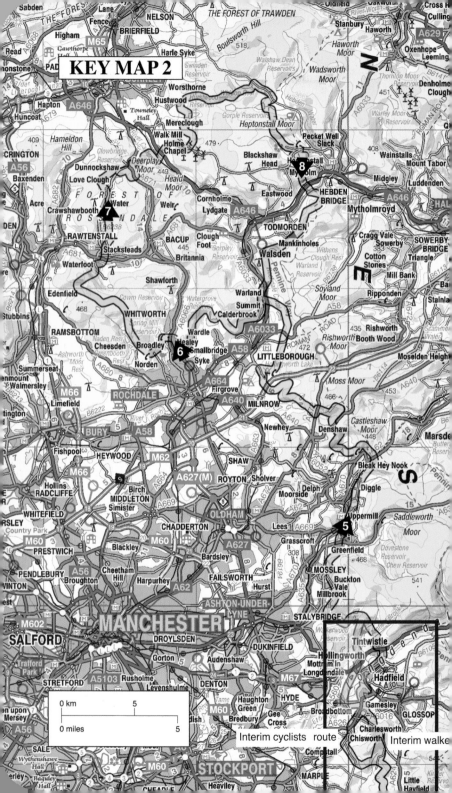

KEY MAP 2

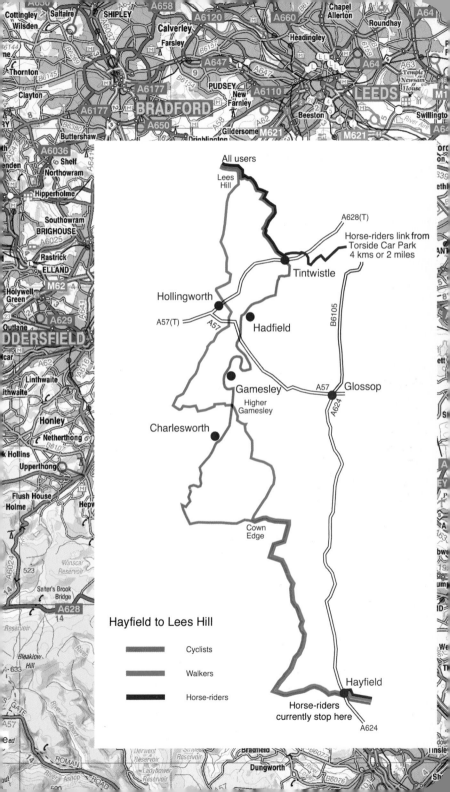

Preface

Welcome to the Pennine Bridleway National Trail, one of the family of 15 National Trails in England and Wales.

This book covers the first part of the Pennine Bridleway National Trail, from Middleton Top or Hartington in Derbyshire up to and including the Mary Towneley Loop. Lady Mary Towneley campaigned for this long-distance 'flagship' riding route along the Pennines and the 47-mile (75.6-km) 'Mary Towneley Loop' was named in her honour by the Princess Royal before Mary sadly died in 2001, after a long and bravely fought illness.

This first section offers wonderful opportunities for riders, cyclists and walkers to enjoy the southern part of the Pennines using a safe, well waymarked (with the acorn mark), largely off-road route, with easy-to-use gates and safe road-crossing points. The route offers a variety of experiences, from old railway lines to open, heather moorland and pretty walled lanes. There are plenty of challenges along the way as the trail crosses the hills of the Peak District National Park and weaves up and down the steep sided valleys of the South Pennines – a good level of fitness is required for mountain bikers, riders and their horses! There is also much historical interest as parts of the Trail follow the ancient packhorse trade routes linking mill towns and villages.

The creation of the Pennine Bridleway has been made possible with the financial support of Sport England and the hard work of the local authorities – our partners in developing and maintaining the Trail.

Suffice to say – whatever your mode of transport have a good time!

Ewen Cameron
Chairman
Countryside Agency

PART ONE

Introduction

The Pennine Bridleway leads through a great range of landscapes: typical White Peak drystone walls and flower-filled meadows, with dark High Peak moorland beyond.

A new concept

The 117-mile (188-km) southern section of the Pennine Bridleway National Trail, running from the High Peak Trail in Derbyshire northwards through the Peak District to the South Pennines on the Lancashire–Yorkshire border, is a long-distance route with a difference. Not only is it the first National Trail designed specifically to cater for the needs of horse-riders and off-road cyclists as well as walkers, it is also the first to include a significant circular section – the 47-mile (75.6-km) Mary Towneley Loop, which at present concludes the Pennine Bridleway – providing a unique and convenient facility for those users who wish to travel from place to place and return to their starting point. Plans are afoot to extend the route north from the Loop to finish at Byrness in Northumberland, a total distance of around 350 miles (560 km).

A varied landscape

The Pennine Bridleway runs through fantastically diverse countryside, starting in the White Peak area of Derbyshire. Over 300 million years ago, in Carboniferous times, the area known today as the Peak District was covered by a shallow tropical sea. The limestone plateau of the White Peak – which is as much as 2,000 feet (600 metres) deep – represents the fossilised remains of thousands of millions of tiny sea creatures, laid down over an incredible 35 million years. At the end of the final glacial period (in Pleistocene times) around 10,000 years ago, fast-flowing meltwaters cut steep-sided valleys through the limestone layer, creating the beautiful dales for which the White Peak is renowned.

Lying around three sides of the White Peak is a horseshoe-shaped band of resistant millstone grit and shales, forming the higher country of the Dark or High Peak. There is a visible division between these two predominant rock types that even those who are not the slightest bit excited by geology cannot fail to notice as the Pennine Bridleway drops down towards Peak Forest. The classic scenery of the White Peak – small, evenly stone–walled fields and green pastures, incised by deep, wooded limestone dales – here gives way to the great swell of the High Peak – dark, powerful, gritstone moorland – that rises to the north of the Manchester–Sheffield road.

The Pennine Bridleway then moves north along the western edge of the South Pennines, overlooking the Tame Valley. As the Peak District is left behind, a second area of rolling gritstone moorland hoves into view – the moors of Rossendale and Calderdale. The Peak District – said to be within one hour's drive of 60 per cent of the population – is commonly described as the 'lung' of England, but there is a smaller, less advertised 'lung' lying further north, straddling the boundary between East Lancashire and West Yorkshire. Easily missed on a small-scale map or road atlas – where it appears to be completely carved up by major roads – this area of the South Pennines (hemmed in between Burnley, Halifax and Rochdale) comprises remote moorland with steep-sided, wooded river valleys. A good scattering of reservoirs, originally constructed to service the canals and needs of the developing industrial cities of the north, add variety to the landscape. Criss-crossed by a fantastic network of old packhorse routes, some dating back to medieval times, this area also has a remarkable industrial heritage, visible today in the form of derelict mills, dismantled railways, soot-blackened gritstone walls and tall, ivy-covered chimneys.

This is the landscape explored by the Pennine Bridleway's Mary Towneley Loop, linked to the linear route at Summit in the Calder Valley. Opened in May 2002, the Loop represents the culmination of many years' hard work and determination on the part of one woman: Lady Mary Towneley, who lived at Dyneley Hall near Holme Chapel, just $^1/_2$ mile (0.8 km) off the route. She campaigned long and hard for a long-distance riding route of some kind, and without her inspiration the Pennine Bridleway would probably not have happened. Mary Towneley rode part of the proposed Loop with HRH The Princess Royal in 2000, but sadly did not live to see its opening; she died from cancer in February 2001. A most appropriate and understated stone memorial, engraved with a horse's head, stands by the route at the top of what she called 'Heartbreak Hill' – on the slopes of Stone House Edge above the Cliviger Valley.

Tackling the Pennine Bridleway

The Pennine Bridleway is a tremendously satisfying route. Not only does it traverse a great variety of landscapes, it also explores some pretty remote areas of the country, but is well signposted and much is along easily followed packhorse trails, so route finding is not a problem. The surfaces underfoot vary from tarmac lanes to stone-setted ways to specially constructed

The track descending into Roych Clough on the edge of the Kinder plateau has been restored and made suitable for all groups of user.

paths, including grassy stretches, over rough moorland. There are quiet lanes and well-surfaced tracks where cyclists will be able to push on, but on the whole this is not a route that can be tackled at speed.

A huge amount of work has gone into rendering the route suitable for the three groups of users. New bridlegates have been installed, bridges and fords constructed, Pegasus and other road crossings built, sections of badly eroded and damaged track restored. It should be relatively easy to follow in all weathers, but it would be sensible to avoid the depths of winter and cold, wet conditions. Try to tackle the Dark Peak, and the Rossendale and Calderdale sections, in particular, in decent weather. Annual rainfall on the Kinder plateau is up to 65 inches (1,630 mm), and on the Rossendale moors the figure is even higher. You are unlikely to get lost – the route is clearly marked – but if you pick a wet, misty day you will certainly miss out on spectacular views and won't have much fun.

There's nothing on the Pennine Bridleway that should deter a competent rider. If you plan to tackle the whole route, check the condition of your tack before you leave: you don't want a broken rein or similar when you're a couple of days out. Make sure you can carry what you need comfortably and securely – a saddlebag is a better option than a rucksack. Some farms and accommodation along the route offer a luggage transporting facility, which is a real advantage: think about your – and your horse's – requirements before booking accommodation. It would be wise to carry an equiboot or similar in case your horse is unlucky enough to cast a shoe. Riders should build up their own and their horses' fitness levels over a number of weeks before starting.

The route itself shouldn't pose any real difficulties. There are a large number of gates to be negotiated, but many are long-handled bridlegates to make opening and closing easy from horseback. Those unused to long days in the saddle can opt for shorter sections; those who have little experience of riding up and down steep hills may find some parts of the route 'exciting', but not impossible. Speed merchants may be disappointed by the lack of long, level, grassy stretches where they can have a good canter. But the Pennine Bridleway provides a fantastic, and flexible, opportunity for keen horse-riders to get right away from it all on a purpose-built route through a fascinating part of the country. **NB Five miles (8 km) north of Hayfield there is a stretch that is not yet open to horses – see page 68 – but advice is given on how to get over the problem, and the Countryside Agency hopes that a suitable route for horse-riders will be set up by 2006.**

It probably doesn't need to be said, but walkers should wear decent boots and carry all their needs for the day – including a good set of breathable waterproofs – in a comfortable rucksack. Take a fleece, even in summer: if the weather closes in and the wind gets up body temperature can drop surprisingly fast. Hat and gloves are a must at all other times of the year. It's always a good idea to carry a compass; although not strictly necessary on a waymarked route such as this, it weighs almost nothing and you never know when you might need to use it. All users should carry sufficient food and drink for the day, as well as a mobile phone and personal first aid kit: if something goes wrong and you need help you can't rely on meeting other people on the route. Although in practice you are never very far from civilisation, there are sections that feel extremely lonely – especially over the Calderdale moors – and it may be that the nearest house or settlement is still 2 or 3 miles away.

Cycling specifics

Anyone planning to tackle the Pennine Bridleway should use a genuine mountain bike. If you haven't already got one, go to a good bike shop and make sure that you get the right advice in terms of both the type and size of bike to go for. The sort of terrain experienced on the route means that you will need decent suspension and brakes – 'V' brakes are more than adequate if you're careful on steep descents – and you will certainly need good all-round tyres, with a reasonable knobbly tread. If you're not used to long days in the saddle, get some practice first and think carefully about how far you want to go each day. Make sure that any accommodation you book for yourself has secure accommodation for your bike too.

Check your bike over before you go, or get it serviced, and think about how much gear you need to take, and how you're going to carry it. A light rucksack or seatpost-mounted bag are probably the best options. Take a puncture repair kit with you, and a couple of spare tubes, as well as a multi-tool so that you can effect minor adjustments en route. It's also a good idea to

Cyclists can enjoy a variety of terrain on the Pennine Bridleway, including moorland tracks such as this one above Widdop Reservoir.

Gritstone outcrops, big skies and wide open spaces: the Calderdale Moors on the northern p

he Mary Towneley Loop.

carry a spare block, and spare brake and gear cable, plus a small tube of lubricant.

Finally, a helmet is essential. Gloves will make your day more comfortable both in terms of keeping your hands warm on cold days and providing padding where your hands rest on the handlebars. Close-fitting stretchy leggings or tracksuit bottoms are suitable; avoid anything baggy that may catch on gears and chains. Wear a shoe with a firm sole; a lightweight walking boot is ideal.

Rules of the road

Users of the Pennine Bridleway should be aware at all times that they are not the only people who want to enjoy the trail, and that consideration should be given to other users, whatever their chosen mode of transport. Cyclists are asked to cycle in control, particularly when going downhill and/or when it is not possible to see that the route ahead is clear; to overtake in single file; and to keep left when passing others approaching in the opposite direction. Cyclists are also requested to ring their bells or call a warning in good time when approaching walkers and horse-riders from behind, and to give horses as wide a berth as possible.

Horses deserve special attention, too. Those people unused to the whys and wherefores of equines are often surprised at how flighty and easily startled they can be. Non-horsey people tend to know to avoid the front and back 'end' – being all too aware of the potential dangers of teeth and hooves – but it is also worth bearing in mind that some horses will be wary of the sight of a mass of cyclists coming towards them, particularly at speed, or may jump at the sound of screeching brakes; many horses will even give a walker wearing a rucksack a wide berth: it's not a sight that horses necessarily come across very often. By the same token, horse-riders should take care not to 'hog' any of the tracks by riding two or three abreast unless there really is a decent amount of room, and should not canter unless they have good visibility ahead and can see that the coast is clear. Some other trail users could be intimidated by the presence of horses.

Both cyclists and horse-riders should also consider the slowest group of users, the walkers, and pass them with care. Walkers can help by stepping aside to allow faster trail users to pass. The basic message is that all users should think about the needs of others on the trail, and give them due consideration.

This fine memorial to Lady Mary Towneley forms a fitting tribute to her tireless enthusiasm for the creation of a long-distance bridleway.

The Mary Towneley Loop

The Mary Towneley Loop was the first part of the Pennine Bridleway to open, in May 2002, so it is worth having a look at how it has developed over the first couple of years. Since its opening, the Loop has become increasingly popular, especially with horse-riders keen to take a break from their normal riding country and share a new experience with their horses. One of the most satisfying aspects of owning a horse is the relationship that builds up between horse and rider over the years – there really is nothing more rewarding than being able to take your horse on holiday with you! Horses enjoy new sensations and experiences just as much as their riders, and the Mary Towneley Loop has filled a real 'gap in the market'. The route is sufficiently 'safe' in terms of terrain and navigation to suit those slightly tentative riders who would not be happy trekking across open unsigned moorland, yet at the same time is challenging enough for the more confident. It's also quite something to be able to ride out from your overnight accommodation straight onto the bridleway, without having to trail along miles of road to get there, and to ride the Loop with a real sense of purpose.

Cyclists too will enjoy the varied off-road terrain. Many users view the Loop in a rather different way to the horse-riding fraternity: some treat the Loop as a one-day challenge ride. However, you should be aware that it is a hilly route and you need to be fit to do it in one day. A two- or three-day cycle is more appropriate for those wanting to enjoy the scenery! Whatever your mode of transport, being able to return to your start point offers a huge advantage – and gives a great sense of achievement – over any linear route, removing the need for that sometimes tedious journey back to wherever you left your car or horsebox.

The creation of the Mary Towneley Loop has also given a real boost to the economy of this part of the South Pennines after the devastating foot-and-mouth outbreak of 2001. The Loop has provided the chance for farms to diversify and provide accommodation for users and, in some cases, horses too, in an area that is not traditionally promoted for tourists. Some local farms on or near the route now offer bed and breakfast and a very welcome luggage-transfer service.

Facilities

The Pennine Bridleway as a whole is not well serviced with refreshment stops en route; by its very nature it keeps well away from the traditional honeypot sites in the Peak District, and most of its course in the South Pennine area is through pretty remote landscapes. Although a few accessible pubs are passed, some may not be open at lunchtimes. On the other hand, there are some that have welcomed the creation of the route, and do provide temporary accommodation for horses in terms of paddocks or hitching rails. See page 163 for details. The overall message here, however, is that all users should plan ahead, check out the facilities, and carry food and drink with them. Horse-riders may also wish to consider carrying a collapsible bucket to collect water for their horses – although watering points are available, in hot conditions additional water may be required.

For accommodation and tourist information, details of farriers, tack shops, cycle hire and repairs, car parks and trail facilities, see Useful Information (pages 157–68).

PART TWO

PENNINE BRIDLEWAY

Derbyshire to the South Pennines

1 Middleton Top/Hartington to Parsley Hay

11¹/₂ miles (18.5 km)/2 miles (3.2 km)

To avoid overcrowding and general confusion at the start of the Pennine Bridleway, the route has been set up so that off-road cyclists and horse-riders wishing to follow the trail from start to finish commence from different places. Cyclists are recommended to start from Middleton Top, near Middleton-by-Wirksworth, in Derbyshire, where they set off along the High Peak Trail. Horse-riders, on the other hand, should start from the old Hartington station on the Tissington Trail, where there are purpose-built facilities for them. Walkers have a choice of starting from either terminus. The High Peak and Tissington Trails join south of Parsley Hay, 11¹/₂ miles (18.5 km) from Middleton Top, and just 2 miles (3.2 km) from Hartington. Within their respective boundaries, the trails are owned and managed by the Peak District National Park Authority and Derbyshire County Council. Utilising the trackbeds of the disused Cromford and High Peak and Ashbourne–Buxton Railways respectively, they opened to the public in 1971.

This will not be a challenging day: the trail is broad and level, and walkers starting from Middleton Top may find the many long, straight stretches (often through deep cuttings) monotonous – but there are some scenic highlights. At certain times, in particular at weekends and in school holidays, large numbers of people hire cycles from Mapleton Lane (on the Tissington Trail), Middleton Top or Parsley Hay, intent on enjoying the delights of off-road cycling for a few hours. The cycle hire at Parsley Hay – where horses using the Pennine Bridleway and cyclists will meet for the first time – is especially busy. Users are advised to try to avoid these times, or to take this section steadily when it is crowded. Anyone embarking on the Pennine Bridleway as a whole will just have to be patient and look forward to the less 'populated' days to come. Having said that, the landscape around this part of the route becomes increasingly pretty and the trails have a fascinating history; all users would be well advised to pursue a leisurely pace and spend some time thinking about the industrial origins of the route.

Middleton Top to Parsley Hay

The Pennine Bridleway joins the already established High Peak Trail at Middleton Top, where there are parking facilities and a picnic area, cycle hire, refreshments, toilets and an excellent information centre. It's a popular spot: approximately 11,000 people pass through the information centre each year, and it is estimated that two and a half times that number actually use the trail.

Originally the line of the Cromford and High Peak Railway, the High Peak Trail today runs for 17½ miles (28 km) from High Peak Junction to Dow Low, 6 miles (9.7 km) south of Buxton. The line was closed to all traffic in 1967 – there's a nostalgic photograph of the locomotive *Journey's End* in April of that year at Longcliffe on the trail. Today it provides a fantastic, safe facility for cyclists and walkers of all ages, virtually without gradients (other than the Hopton Incline, which comes early on) and well supplied with information boards, picnic areas and easily accessed car parks.

Before setting out, have a look around Middleton Top – there's a mass of information here on the industrial history of what is, today, a great leisure attraction. The Cromford and High Peak Railway, opened in 1830, was one of the world's first long-distance railways, and was designed to link two canals – the Cromford Canal and the High Peak Canal. The original intention was to construct a canal to link Nottinghamshire and Derbyshire to the industrial north-west, but the terrain of the southern Peak District proved too severe; even so, the railway was designed on canal-like lines. There are nine inclines on its course, raising the track more than 950 feet (300 metres) from High Peak Junction to its highest point near Buxton – quite a feat for any railway. In the early days horses were used to pull wagons carrying coal or stone along the level sections of track; later, steam locomotives took over. The engine house **1** at the top of Middleton Incline houses the oldest known working rotating-beam engine (in its original position) – the Middleton Top engine, built in 1829 – which for 133 years raised and lowered wagons up or down the incline. The term 'hanger on' originates from these times, and was the name given to the man who attached chains to the wagons so that they could be hauled up the incline. The engine can still be seen in action on Bank Holidays and on the first weekend of each month from April to October.

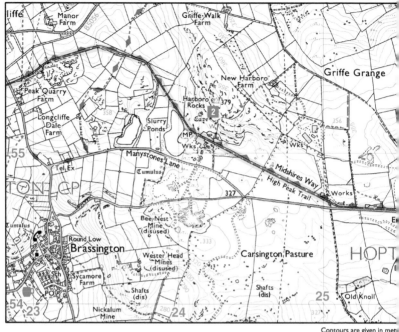

Contours are given in met
The vertical interval is 5m

The start of the trail is easy to find **A**: turn left from the car park and information centre, and follow the broad, level track, which soon passes disused Intake Quarry on the right. The village of Middleton, lying just to the south of the Peak District National Park boundary, is surrounded by a number of active limestone quarries, producing stone for road building and concrete aggregate. Between Middleton and larger Wirksworth – at one time one of the most important towns in Derbyshire on account of its lead-mining industry – can be found the National Stone Centre. Anyone wishing to have a deeper understanding of the make-up of the Derbyshire landscape would be well advised to spend some time here.

Pass through a bridlegate, across a track, and through another gate. Hopton Tunnel, in a deep cutting, hoves into view; once through the tunnel look back towards deeply scarred Middleton Moor to the north of the trail – you'll get a better understanding of the scale of the quarrying in the area. The trail soon rises steadily up the long Hopton Incline (1:14); pass through the bridlegate at the top of the slope to reach Hopton Top, where there are picnic tables and a sculpture. This remarkably steep incline – for an engine, at least – caused all sorts of

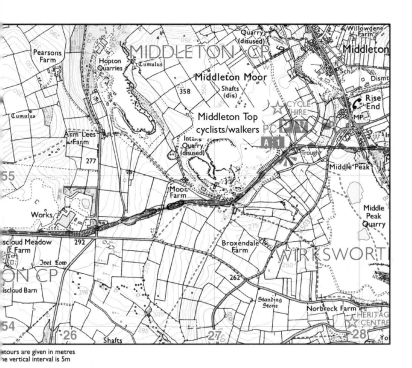

Contours are given in metres
The vertical interval is 5m

problems to locomotives, but today's users will make little of it. When the London & North Western Railway took over the line in 1877 the Hopton winding engine, which used to haul wagons up the incline, was removed and locomotives had to climb under their own steam, sometimes needing several attempts to reach the top: it must have been quite a sight! The gradient was eased in 1903, but the incline was still the steepest gradient worked regularly by conventional steam locomotives on British railways.

There's a cottage on the right of the track at Hopton Top; look out too for the black-and-white photographs of former railway employees which can be found on the side of the small shed on the right – and particularly for Frank 'Hellfire' Brown! Note too the stone-built remains of an old windmill in the fields to the left of the trail. The trail continues between stone walls to cross the tarmac lane leading to New Harboro Farm, and through a bridlegate. A footpath left leads to the village of Carsington and Carsington Water, a reservoir opened in 1992 with facilities for all kinds of watersports, as well as walking, cycling, fishing and birdwatching. The trail crosses the footpath leading to Brassington (where there is a pub) to the left, and Harboro Rocks **2** – a rugged limestone outcrop, rising to 1,243 feet (379 metres) –

soon appears above right, giving an inkling of the landscape features to come. Artefacts dating from late Palaeolithic to medieval times have been excavated from a large cave here.

The trail continues through gently rolling farmland to run parallel to the B5056 as Longcliffe, with its calcium carbonate works, is approached. The trail crosses the Longcliffe–Brassington road and bears sharp right, passing a disused quarry and ruined building on the left: this is the site of the old Longcliffe goods yard, once important for transporting limestone, and milk from local farms, now home to picnic tables and the odd sculpture. It was also an essential watering place, water not being in great supply locally on account of the porous qualities of the underlying limestone. Spring water was brought here in tenders from Cromford to supply steam locomotives and other industrial and domestic purposes in the locality.

Cross the B5056 on a bridge and continue on to Hoe Grange, at which point the Peak District National Park – the first to be designated, in 1951 – is quietly entered **B**. Continue on, with views over Ballidon and Hoe Grange Quarries to the left. Look ahead right to see a wooded hillock, rising to 1,220 feet (372 metres);

Typical views early on the trail may not be dramatic, but are certainly easy on the eye.

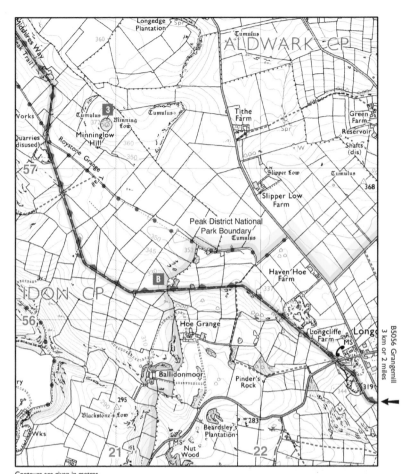

Contours are given in metres
The vertical interval is 5m

just beyond lies the course of a Roman road that ran from Derby to Buxton. This is Minninglow Hill **3**, on which stands a Neolithic chambered tomb, now surrounded by a clump of beech trees. Although little evidence has been found of the domestic activities of these early farmers (dating from 4500 to 2000 BC), the White Peak has a good scattering of burial cairns and henges. The most significant is the Neolithic henge monument at Arbor Low, near Parsley Hay. Dating from 3000 BC, Arbor Low is contemporary with the more nationally famous megalithic structure at Stonehenge in Wiltshire.

The next point of interest comes soon after, where Gallowlow Lane, part of the Roystone Grange Trail, crosses the trail from the right. Gallowlow Lane may date from Roman times; it is certainly at least medieval. The Roystone Grange area provides an excellent example of a pattern of continuous occupation from prehistoric times to the present day. There is evidence of Neolithic and Bronze Age farming activity, the Neolithic chambered tomb on Minninglow Hill, and a Bronze Age barrow, from which a number of skulls – without bodies – have been excavated. Orthostat walls – where large stones (orthostats) form the foundation layer, with courses of small stones above – have been dated to the 2nd century AD, when Romano-British peoples farmed here and enclosed the land. The Roman field system can still be seen towards Ballidon. Roystone 4 and Minninglow 5 Granges were post-medieval farmsteads, owned by the Cistericians in the 12th or 13th centuries. Later came the Victorian quarries, limekilns and brickworks and, of course, the railway cut through the middle of it all in 1830.

Follow the trail on through a five-bar gate and a small cutting. Soon after, it runs over first Roystone and then Minninglow embankments. These are approximately 20 feet (6 metres) wide, with a drop of 40 feet (12 metres) and low (18-inch/0.5-metre) stone parapets. Consequently notices recommend that cyclists should stop and give way to other users, dogs be kept on leads, and small children supervised. The trail passes a disused working on the right, then swings left to cross the Grade II listed Minninglow embankment, built circa 1825. The views here on either side of the trail are becoming increasingly open and pretty, with small walled fields. The track too has wide verges here, forming valuable and relatively undisturbed 'corridors' for wildflowers and wildlife. In spring look out for cowslips in particular; in summer you will see bird's-foot trefoil, scabious, vetches, wild strawberry and small, low-growing carpets of wild thyme.

Pass round a gate, cross a quiet lane, and go through another gate to reach the car park and picnic area at Minninglow. The trail proceeds over a lane on a bridge and under the ash and sycamore trees of Chapel Plantation (a welcome relief on a hot day). Once out of the trees, a farm track is crossed before the trail veers steeply right at Gotham Curve (the tightest curve on any main line railway at the time it was built). The next stretch is long, straight and embanked, before the trail curves left away from the hamlet of Pikehall on the A5012, which can be seen across fields to the right. Look left to see an old walled green lane passing under the railway line. Continue straight on to Newhaven Crossing; go through a bridlegate (this is a busy road – take care) and cross the road **C**;

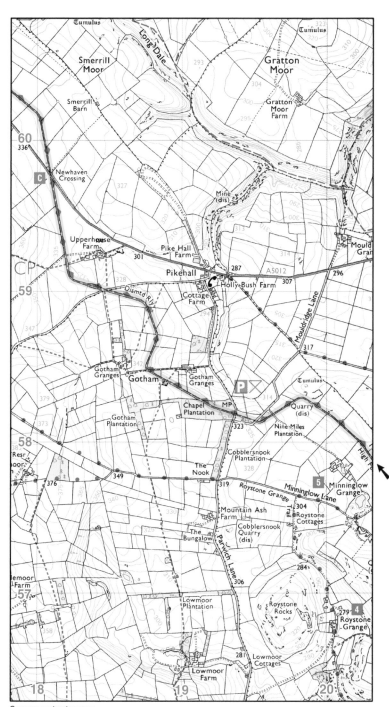

Contours are given in metres
The vertical interval is 5m

33

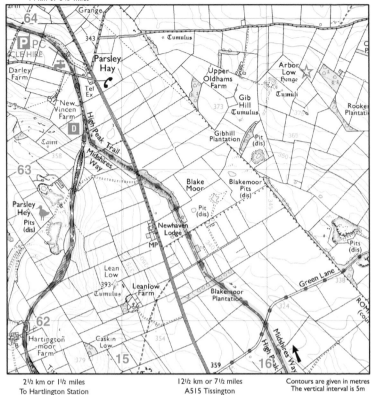

2½ km or 1½ miles
To Hartlington Station

12½ km or 7½ miles
A515 Tissington

Contours are given in metres
The vertical interval is 5m

turn left on a gritty track and go through another gate to regain the trail. Two long, straight sections – cyclists can push on safely here – lead to the gate into the picnic area and car park at Friden.

Cross the lane to pass the back wall of the brickworks **6** on the left; pause for a while to read the information boards here, and admire the murals, put up in 2001 by retired employees. Friden brickworks opened in 1892. Volcanic activity in the area millions of years ago formed deposits of ganister, a stone with a high silica content, suitable for the production of high-quality heat-resistant bricks, using local sand and clay. These raw materials were dug out by hand and brought to the works by horse-drawn wagon. The high-grade silica bricks were used the world over in gas retort systems, for the production of town gas; when natural gas was found in the North Sea demand rapidly diminished. The horse-drawn wagons were dropped in the 1930s in favour of narrow-gauge locomotives on the Cromford and High Peak line; motorised transport came in during the 1940s, and the last train ran through the site in 1965. Something else that changed over the years was the source of raw materials; by 2001 all major materials were imported by ship and road from all over the world.

Continue along the trail, over a farm track and through a bridlegate. A long straight section follows, crossing the farm track leading to Brundcliffe Farm on the right, and through another gate. Another long straight section crosses a green lane, passes through a bridlegate to enter narrow Blakemoor Plantation, and then over a lane through two rows of low posts. Continue through a cutting – note the old signal post on the left – and under a bridge, before passing through Newhaven Tunnel under the A515. Emerge from the cutting to reach the junction with the Tissington Trail, which joins from the left **D**. Things may start to get a little busier here, with walkers, cyclists and horse-riders joining the High Peak Trail. A notice-board reveals that the Tissington Trail starts at Ashbourne, 13$\frac{1}{2}$ miles (21.7 km) away. Continue on to cross a road on a bridge; the cycle hire, car park, toilets, picnic area and refreshments at Parsley Hay will be found on the right of the trail. Parsley Hay – one of the first cycle-hire centres in the country (it opened in 1975) – was once a busy station and goods yard, serving the local rural population.

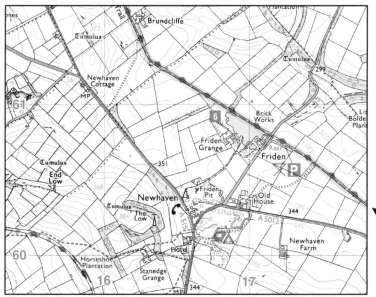

A515 Buxton
17 km or 10½ miles

Contours are given in metres
The vertical interval is 5m

Hartington to Parsley Hay

New facilities for horses and their owners have been developed at Hartington station, 2 miles (3.2 km) south of Parsley Hay on the old Ashbourne–Buxton line. There is a large dedicated parking area for horseboxes, a small paddock, hitching posts, access to water and a shelter. The signal box is open for inspection; there are refreshments, toilets, information and a picnic area. The Ashbourne–Buxton railway line opened in 1899 and was closed in 1962; as well as coping with goods trains Hartington was a popular stopping-off point for tourists aiming 'For Dove Dale, Beresford Dale and the Manifold Valley', as still displayed on the side of the restored signal box. The regular passenger service stopped in 1954. The attractive nearby village of Hartington **7**, situated near the head of Dove Dale and a market since 1203, is particularly well known as the only remaining place in Derbyshire where Stilton cheese is 'officially' made; the other source is the Vale of Belvoir in Leicestershire. Hartington Creamery was set up in the 1870s, and began making Stilton cheese in the 1920s. The church dates from the 14th century, and the village also boasts the oldest Youth Hostel in the Peak District, opened in 1934. The two pubs in Hartington – The Devonshire Arms and The Charles Cotton – are both named for local figures. Successive Dukes of Devonshire have been resident at Chatsworth – the 'Palace of the Peak' – near Edensor, east of the Derwent Valley, for some 400 years. Charles Cotton lived in Beresford Dale and was a companion of Izaak Walton. The pair extolled the qualities of fishing the White Peak rivers, including the Dove; today Dove Dale is the most popular dale, visited by more than 1 million people every year. Cotton and Walton, who co-authored *The Compleat Angler* in 1652, would have been amazed. Cotton later wrote *The Wonders of the Peake*, published in 1681 and still in print.

Hartington makes a very attractive setting-off point for those on horseback, and – for walkers, who have a choice here – is scenically more satisfying than the early parts of the High Peak Trail. On leaving the station **E**, heading north, beautiful wide views over Long Dale and towards Hartington open up almost immediately to the left. Again the track is broad and gritty, with wide verges, although cantering is not possible. Follow the trail as it leads gently through the rolling landscape to pass through a deep cutting and join the High Peak Trail just south of Parsley Hay. At this point horse-riders should become increasingly vigilant and be on the look out for cyclists.

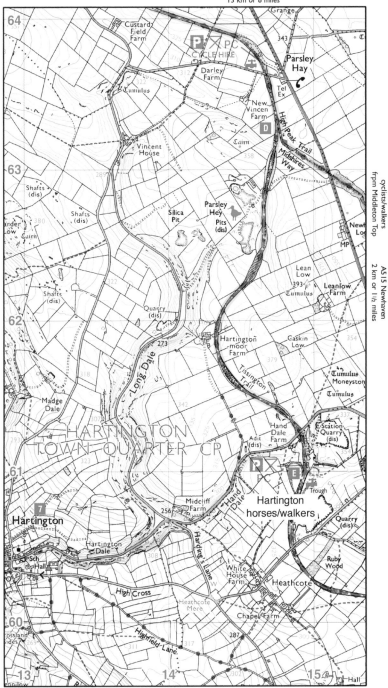

Contours are given in metres
The vertical interval is 5m

Arkwright and the birth of the Industrial Revolution

It is appropriate that a long-distance bridleway that later on its course runs through so much of the old industrial heart of the country – the South Pennine valleys – should begin so near the site of 'where it all began'. It can be said that the Industrial Revolution really started at Cromford – originally a small medieval village – just a couple of miles away from Middleton Top in the Derwent Valley.

Hard on the heels of James Hargreaves' invention of the hand-powered Spinning Jenny in 1764 – thereby increasing the number of threads that could be spun at one time, by one person – came Richard Arkwright's water-powered Water Frame. Arkwright – known as 'the father of the factory system' – started to build the world's first successful water-powered cotton mill at Cromford in 1771. The local lead-mining industry, dating back to pre-Roman times, was in decline, so labour was cheap and available; water power from the fast-flowing Bonsall Brook (and, later, the River Derwent) was plentiful. Hand spinning and weaving had until that time been carried out in the home, but the innovative Arkwright broke the mould: as well as constructing a second mill in 1783 – the Masson Mill – he built houses and facilities for his employees, thereby setting up a model industrial village. Others would follow his example all over the world. He also built the church, in which he lies buried. Textile production at Cromford Mill stopped in 1840 because of water supply problems – the cotton industry was in decline in Derbyshire by this time – but both Cromford Mill and Masson Mill are open to the public today. Cromford Mill has been designated as the Derwent Valley World Heritage Site.

Arkwright's Cromford Mill stands at the head of the Cromford Canal (which can also be accessed via the High Peak Trail – turn right from Middleton Top and follow the trail down the Middleton Incline to High Peak Junction). The canal was completed in 1794, and ran for 14$\frac{1}{2}$ miles (23 km) to Langley Mill, where it joined the Erewash Canal. In 1830 it was linked to the Peak Forest Canal at Whaley Bridge, north of Buxton, via the Cromford and High Peak Railway. Today there is still water in the canal for the 5-mile (8-km) stretch from Cromford south to Ambergate, and the site provides an opportunity for leisure activities; it is also a Site of Special Scientific Interest on account of its rich flora and fauna. Visitors can see the 1849 beam engine at the restored Leawood pump house.

The splendid Middleton Top engine, built in 1839, is housed in the restored engine house at the top of Middleton Incline, and is occasionally open to the public.

2 Parsley Hay to Peak Forest

16 miles (25.7 km)

Today is 'White Peak' day. The route of the Pennine Bridleway traverses the lofty Carboniferous Limestone plateau of the southern Peak District, lying around 1,000 feet (300 metres) above sea level, a landscape characterised by rolling pastures, regimented stone-walled fields, steep-sided wooded dales – and a great feeling of space. There are fabulous areas of natural limestone grassland supporting a wide variety of flowers and butterflies during spring and summer. The Pennine Bridleway keeps far away from the beaten track, using ancient tracks and deserted lanes, passing remote farms and cottages. Note that there is little chance of refreshment or supplies on the route itself, but occasional brief detours to pubs or villages are possible. It's almost impossible to believe that the Peak District National Park receives an estimated 22 million visitors a year – you will see very few of them on today's route! Horse-riders should note that at the time of writing the only way to cross the River Wye in Chee Dale is via a 3-foot- (1-metre)-wide, 100-feet- (30-metre)-long timber-decked footbridge. The bridge has three shallow timber steps on the approach, but has been used by horses. It is anticipated that an additional horse-friendly

The sympathetically restored signal box at Hartington station: an attractive starting point for horse-riders.

bridge will be installed during 2004. Horses can access the river to drink, but fording is not recommended.

On leaving Parsley Hay **A,** notices announce that it is only 2 1/2 miles (4 km) to the end of the trail, and the 'drop-off' rate of casual cyclists becomes increasingly apparent as Parsley Hay is left behind. Although the trail immediately around Parsley Hay is busy, this final stretch of the High Peak Trail appears to be less popular than the trails from either Middleton Top or Ashbourne to Parsley Hay, which seem to provide the focus for many users. The trail north of Parsley Hay is broad and open, with wide grassy verges; Cotesfield Farm is passed on the right, after which the trail runs through a cutting and under a bridge. Continue on

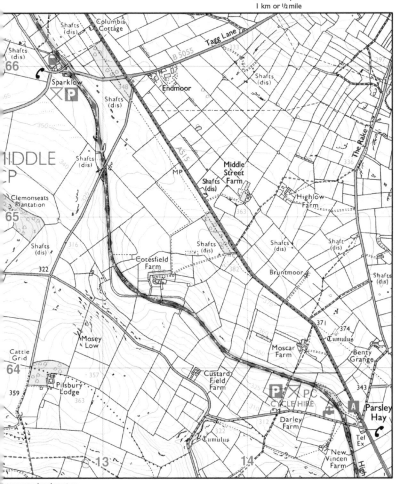

B5005 Monyash
1 km or 1/2 mile

ntours are given in metres
he vertical interval is 5m

to cross a minor road; the A515 can be seen across fields to the right, with the line of an old Roman road running parallel to it. Continue through the parking and picnic area at Sparklow (site of the old station and goods yard for Hurdlow on the Cromford and High Peak Railway); The Royal Oak pub is signed just off the route to the left. Keep straight on through a gate and through a cutting under the B5055. This is where things definitely settle down; users seen beyond this point are most likely to be following the Pennine Bridleway. The trail becomes narrower, with wide 'wildlife corridor' verges; to the left can be seen the rounded outline of Cronkston Low **8**, which has a tumulus on top; Hurdlow Grange – one of 50 or so granges (monastic sheep farms) in the Peak District – lies at the foot of the hill. Pass under a substantial bridge (walkers should note that a footpath leading right here goes to The Duke of York pub at Pomeroy), and then another bridge; just after the second one there is access on the right to the caravan and campsite at Street House Farm.

The High Peak Trail ends rather inauspiciously at a five-bar gate at Dow Low **B**; note that the quarry ahead left lies outside the National Park boundary. The line of the Cromford and High Peak Railway would have continued on to Whaley Bridge, and parts of the track beyond this point are still in working order. Turn right along a walled lane to reach the A515; turn right just before the road on a fenced section. The road is very close and slightly above the path; heavy traffic comes along here pretty fast – be warned.

After 100 yards/metres turn left to cross the road **C** – cyclists may like to know that The Duke of York pub **9** (parts of which date from the early 15th century) can be found straight ahead along the A515 – and follow this quiet lane for about $^1/_2$ mile (0.8 km). Where it bends left, keep straight ahead along low-walled Highstool Lane, a green lane. This bears left and drops gently downhill: look left to see the town of Buxton in the distance. Buxton – a spa town since the time of the Romans on account of the restorative qualities of its natural warm springs – has some fine 18th-century buildings resulting from the Duke of Devonshire's intention to develop the town as a rival to other spa towns such as Bath. Buxton today is perhaps best known for its annual Festival of Music and Arts, focused on the splendid Opera House, which opened in 1905. Spring water is still freely available from St Anne's Well. Cross the lane running between Chelmorton and Flagg, and go straight ahead, signed Taddington. This soon bears right; fork left along another green lane, Pillwell Lane. Two bridleways lead off this to the left, signed Chelmorton.

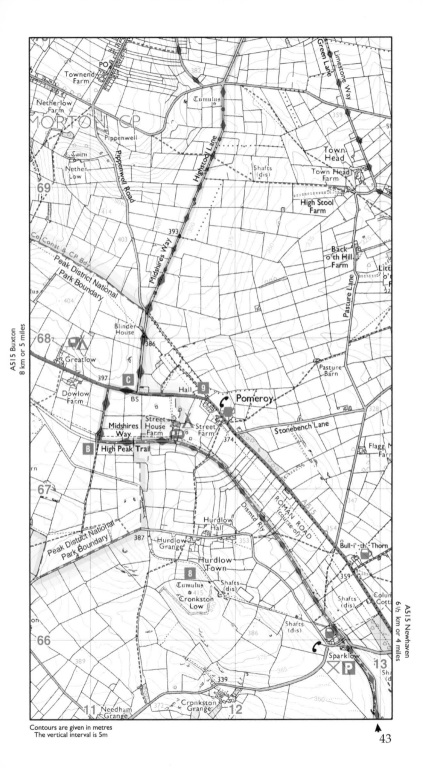

Contours are given in metres
The vertical interval is 5m

This view over Chelmorton clearly shows the exceptionally regimented medieval field system that merits a conservation order on the village and surrounding area.

It's well worth dropping down one of these paths to take a look at this ancient village **10**, nestling 1,100 feet (336 metres) above sea level in a dry valley at the foot of Chelmorton Low **11**, which rises to 1,463 feet (446 metres) and has two tumuli on its summit. You don't even have to go right down into the valley to get a feel for the place: its linear layout and pattern of narrow, low-walled fields can be clearly seen from above. What you're looking at is one of the best examples of a medieval field system in the National Park; the original medieval field pattern was 'preserved' by stone walls after the Field Enclosure Act of 1805. Thankfully the village has not suffered from 20th-century development, and is a conservation area – even the telephone box is a listed building! The church, built on the site of the original 13th-century chantry, has some interesting features too: its unusual weathervane – a golden locust – represents the symbol of St John the Baptist, to whom the church is dedicated. If you do make a detour to the village, stop for a drink at The Church Inn, opposite the church. The village's original water supply, the never-failing 'Illy Willy Water', rises near here too, and for many years ran as an open stream down the main street.

Back on the trail, just beyond the bridleways leading to Chelmorton, Pillwell Lane bears sharp right towards Fivewells Farm; keep straight ahead on a rough green lane to meet five-barred Pillwell Gate, on the edge of the scarp slope. There are good views ahead over the valley of the Wye and the limestone plateau beyond, rising to around 1,000 feet (300 metres). The Five Wells Neolithic chambered cairn **12**, one of the largest (and highest, at around 1,400 feet/427 metres) in the country, lies along the scarp edge to the right of Pillwell Gate. Pass through the gate and follow the grassy track downhill; it bears right and then left to pass a jumble of black-roofed sheds on the left. Pass through a metal gate onto the access road to the former Calton Hill landfill site. Turn right and follow the road, which bears left downhill to meet the A6.

Cross the A6 on the purpose-built crossing, which gives good visibility in both directions. Go straight ahead along a lane signed Blackwell. Where the lane bends sharp right by Cottage Farm, turn left through a gate onto a farm track **D**. Continue

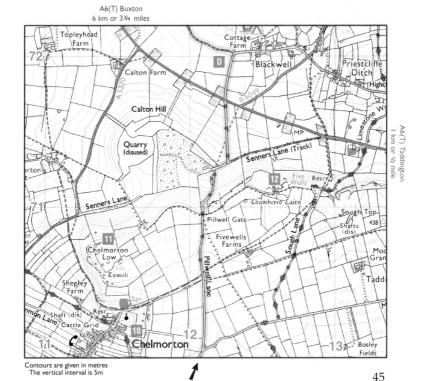

Contours are given in metres
The vertical interval is 5m

along this track through three sets of bridlegates; bear left across the next field to go through another bridlegate. Superb views over Chee Dale **13**, with its lofty limestone buttresses, open up to the right. This spot is popular with climbers. Although this activity is more associated with the hard gritstone edges of the Dark Peak – where rock climbing 'started' as early as the 1890s – in the 1960s and 1970s improved equipment and techniques enabled enthusiasts to turn their attention to the limestone walls and crags of the White Peak. Keep going to the next bridlegate, which leads into Chee Dale Nature Reserve, part of the Wye Valley Site of Special Scientific Interest.

Turn right and follow this lovely, grassy path as it descends gently towards the valley floor. Take care: it can be slippery due to the limestone lying just beneath the grass surface. The sparkling River Wye runs through the valley below, flanked by slopes of ash woodland. This area of limestone grassland is one of the best examples to be found in the Peak District, and is of national importance on account of its wildlife and geology. Look out for cowslips and bright blue Jacob's Ladder in spring; there seem to be butterflies – including the dark green fritillary – everywhere; by the river you may see the charismatic dipper (which has the extraordinary capability of walking underwater along stream and river beds as it searches for food). These wooded limestone dales also hold populations of important summer-visiting migrant birds: the redstart, which comes here from northern Africa; the wood warbler, characterised by its call, an accelerating trill, almost like a spinning coin; and, in areas of sessile oak woodland, the striking black-and-white pied flycatcher. All the regular garden birds can be seen in the dales too – robin, wren, blackbird, great spotted woodpecker and the like – and by the river you may also see grey wagtail and common sandpiper. You may be lucky enough to see a kingfisher flashing by, but you're more likely to spot one if you've identified it by its piping call first.

Where the path bears left over a stile, keep straight ahead through a bridlegate and over a bridge that crosses the old dismantled railway. Above the trail there is a rather confusing Y-shaped junction of railway lines in this valley **14**, where Great Rocks Dale, Wye Dale and Chee Dale meet. The line crossed here is part of the Midland Railway line that ran from St Pancras London–Manchester, constructed in 1860; it's amazing to think that express main line trains used to rush through this beautiful valley. Today it serves a different purpose as the Monsal Trail **15**. This 8½-mile (13.7-km) trail was opened for walkers, cyclists

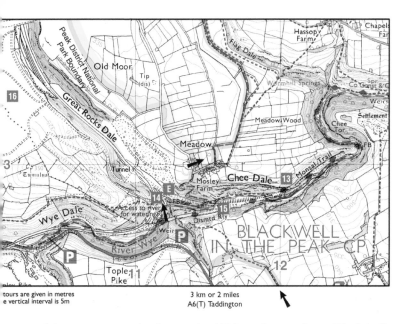

tours are given in metres
e vertical interval is 5m

3 km or 2 miles
A6(T) Taddington

and in some parts for horses in 1980, and runs from Blackwell Mill (east of Buxton) to south of Bakewell, along beautiful wooded Wye Dale, Chee Dale and Miller's Dale.

Follow the track as it bears left then right into a small parking area by a broad, tranquil stretch of the River Wye. This is an idyllic spot, with a delightful terrace – Blackwell Mill Cottages – on the opposite bank. As mentioned earlier, the only way to cross the river at the time of writing is via the footbridge (about 3 feet/1 metre wide and 100 feet/30 metres long), which is usable by horses only with care. A new bridle bridge will be built in 2004. Fording the river is not recommended.

Cross the river and turn right **E** on the other side to pass the Lazy Days tuck shop – ring the bell if you're hungry and no one seems to be around. Follow a narrow path along the left bank of the river: note that in winter this can be very wet. After about 100 yards/metres a small path drops away right along the river bank; at this point bear left uphill away from the river to pass under a railway bridge (under the line that ran into Great Rocks Dale). Follow the path as it zig-zags very steeply uphill, parallel to a drystone wall on the left. As you gain height look down over the junction of dales below. As at Hurdlow, the railway lines just outside the National Park boundary – which the Pennine Bridleway follows on the climb out of Chee Dale – are still used for limestone quarrying: huge quarries **16** flank Great Rocks Dale.

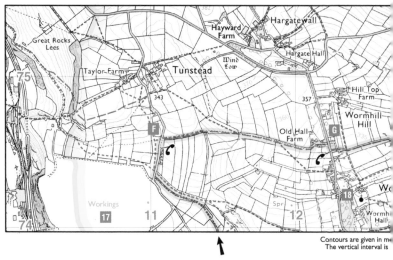

Contours are given in me
The vertical interval is

The grassy path levels off on the approach to Mosley Farm, and becomes walled. Pass through a bridlegate and turn right along a farm track, passing to the left of the farmhouse. Pass a big metal open-sided barn on the right; turn left just before an old barn along a narrow, walled green lane. Follow this to where it ends at a five-bar gate; turn right through a gate and keep along the left edge of the field, with an ash and sycamore plantation left. Pass through a gate on to the lane leading to the farm, and turn left.

Follow this quiet lane – it leads only to Mosley Farm – for about ³/₄ mile (1.2 km); there is a bridleway along the verge. In summer you will come across a fabulous display of meadowsweet and wild geraniums in the verges. This lane eventually joins the lane leading to Tunstead Quarry on the left; turn right. Note that this is a working quarry and blasting can take place at any time between 9am and 4pm on weekdays. Pass farm cottages on the right, and a phone box; about 50 yards/metres later, turn right **F** to leave the lane along a walled and rutted farm track (muddy in winter). Go through the five-bar gate at the end and into a field; keep straight ahead along the bottom edge of the field, keeping the wall on the right. Pass through an open gateway at the end of the field and go straight on, now keeping the wall on the left. Look right here for a good view over the huge limestone workings at Tunstead Quarry **17**.

At the top of the field go through a metal gate and straight on, with the wall on the left. The field levels off and drops down to a metal gate at Old Hall Farm. Keep on downhill, passing stables

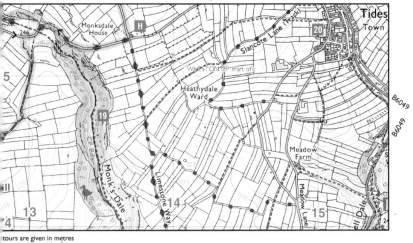

tours are given in metres
e vertical interval is 5m

on the left and the farmhouse right, along the drive to meet a lane on the edge of the little village of Wormhill. This settlement was mentioned in the Domesday Book of 1086, and was a significant place at the time, being an administrative centre for the Royal Forest of the Peak, a hunting ground dating back to the 12th century. Wormhill also has an interesting, and somewhat unexpected, link to a later section of the Pennine Bridleway. The course of the Mary Towneley Loop, which spans the border between East Lancashire and West Yorkshire, runs for a time above the Rochdale Canal. The canal engineer, James Brindley, was originally commissioned to work on the project; he also designed the Trent and Mersey and Chesterfield Canals. He was born in nearby Tunstead in 1716, and there is a memorial to him on the green in Wormhill **18**, erected in 1895.

Turn right along the lane for a few yards, and then left **G** opposite the phone box up a walled track. Pass Elmtree Cottage on the right and continue ahead up a really lovely, grassy, narrow, low-walled green lane that runs gently uphill between the fields. This curves at the top of the hill, goes through a gate, then drops gently downhill under a line of twisted hawthorns. Go through a small gate and downhill – the steep slopes of Monk's Dale **19** appear across the fields ahead. Follow the path as it turns sharp left (with broken-down walls immediately in front of you) and runs downhill to a gate. Pass through that into a field, and go diagonally left downhill to a bridlegate onto a lane.

Turn right down the lane into Monk's Dale. This is part of the Derbyshire Dales National Nature Reserve, and on either

49

Typical Derbyshire dales scenery as the Pennine Bridleway drops towards the junction of

...le and Monk's Dale: ash woodland, hay meadows and limestone walls.

Medieval Wheston Cross stands close to its original location near the centre of the hamlet, and was probably used for 'preaching, public proclamation and penance'.

side of the lane can be seen flower-rich pastures and old woodland. The whole nature reserve – which incorporates five dales – is managed to maintain a suitable environment for plants and wildlife; the woodlands are coppiced, and the grassland grazed by sheep and cattle to maintain the abundance of wild flowers and therefore butterflies. If you're lucky enough to be here in early summer you can see early purple orchids, cowlips, rock rose and thyme, among many other species. It is also believed that a secret tunnel runs from Monk's Dale to the church at Tideswell, but opinion is divided as to its purpose! The lane climbs very steeply out of the dale, passing a stand of beech trees on the right, before levelling off. Where Monk's Dale House appears on the left, with a green lane running away right, turn left along a broad walled lane **H**.

If you are in need of a break don't turn left here, but keep straight ahead along the lane. The lovely village of Tideswell **20** can be found just a mile (1.6 km) away, and is well worth a visit – but it does get busy in the holiday season. Tideswell is perhaps best known for its fabulous 14th-century church of St John the Baptist, popularly known as 'the Cathedral of the Peak' and built in Decorated and Perpendicular styles, with a pinnacled tower. The village was granted a market charter in 1251, and by the 14th century was wealthy on account of the wool trade and lead mining. A popular attraction in many Peak District villages is the annual well-dressing ceremony, when villagers give thanks for their water supply in this dry limestone area, and wells are beautifully decorated with flowers and natural items. Tideswell is no exception. The ceremony is thought to date from Celtic times, but the Christian version originated in Tissington in 1615 when villagers believed that the qualities of their local water had saved them from the Black Death.

If you decide to give Tideswell a miss, continue along the walled lane. You get a real feeling of the limestone plateau here; the fields are divided by drystone walls of uniform height; there are green pastures and sheep, isolated clumps of woodland, and good views over Peter Dale **21** to the left. Where the lane bends right at a clump of sycamore, keep straight ahead on a walled farm track that runs between fields before bearing right and downhill to the hamlet of Wheston, with Top Farm on the right. Meet a tarmac lane and turn left to reach a junction of lanes, with Wheston Hall left. The lane ahead is signed Smalldale; just along this lane stands a wayside cross **22**, dating from medieval times.

Turn right **I** at the junction, and follow this quiet, broad, walled lane for about 1 mile (1.6 km). As Limestone Way Farm

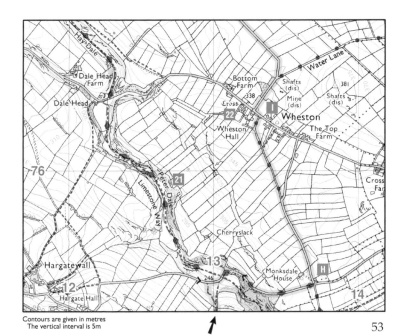

Contours are given in metres
The vertical interval is 5m

comes into view ahead and to the left of the lane, turn left **J** down a walled track. The Pennine Bridleway shares this part of the route with the Limestone Way, which runs for almost 50 miles (80 km) through the classic landscapes of the White Peak from Castleton in the north to Rocester, just over the border into Staffordshire. This track drops steeply downhill, bearing left beneath limestone crags **23** into peaceful Hay Dale (also part of the Derbyshire Dales NNR). There is a lovely clump of hornbeam and ash just inside the reserve, providing a shady spot for two-footed followers of the Pennine Bridleway on a hot day; horses, however, are not allowed into the reserve. Follow the track between walls as it climbs uphill out of the dale to meet a tarmac road.

Early purple orchids – the classic species of White Peak limestone grassland – can be seen in abundance in early summer.

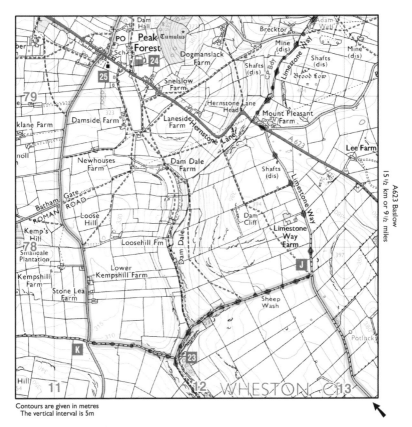

Contours are given in metres
The vertical interval is 5m

Turn right **K** and stay on this road for a rather tedious 1¹/₂ miles (2.4 km). It's not particularly busy, and climbs steadily uphill to pass a road going left; keep straight on to the top of Loose Hill. This is where things definitely improve: as the road drops downhill to join a busier tarmac road on a bend – the line of the road to the left follows an old Roman road – amazing views of the Dark Peak open up ahead, a huge backdrop of dark moorland. It's a stunning sight; the clear division between the softly undulating limestone plateau of the White Peak and the harsh, tough Dark Peak moorland is laid out before you in all its dramatic glory. It really does encourage you to keep moving along this boring stretch. Keep going along the road – which is quite busy – to meet the A623 Stockport/Manchester–Sheffield road at Peak Forest; cross the road via the crossing. The village is somewhat overpowered by lorries thundering along the A623, but does have a pub – The Devonshire Arms **24** – a few yards beyond the crossing point.

'Tow'd man'

There is a long history of mining and quarrying in the Peak District, and copper and lead have been extracted since pre-Roman times. 'Pigs' of lead dating from the Roman period (AD 70–410), inscribed with the word *Lutudarum* – known to have been a site in the Peak District – have been found as far away as Sussex. The industry reached its peak between 1700 and 1750, at which time there were thought to be about 10,000 lead miners. The majority of the local population in the 18th and 19th centuries survived through a combination of farming, spinning and weaving (at home or in the mills), and small-scale mining. A miner was known locally as 't'owd man', and evidence of the industry remains today, mainly in the form of grassed-over hollows and hummocks. Those interested in learning more should try to visit the Magpie Mine near Sheldon, 5 miles (8 km) west of Bakewell just off the A6, the most complete example of a White Peak lead mine. The mine closed in 1953 – the industry died out during the 20th century – and is protected as an ancient monument. Now fluospar and barytes – waste products of lead mining, but essential to today's steel and chemical, and paint and oil industries respectively – is being extracted from some of the old workings. The heyday of copper mining in the Peak District was in the late 18th century, largely at Ecton Hill in the Manifold Valley.

Large-scale quarrying of limestone all along this section of the Pennine Bridleway highlights the whole question of conflicting interests within National Parks. All the way from Middleton Top to Peak Forest such demands are obvious – the underlying limestone is a valuable natural resource for cement and building work, and has significantly influenced the line of the National Park boundary. The Buxton area, for example, is not included within the Peak District National Park because of the large number of limestone quarries in the vicinity. Individual National Park authorities have to perform a constant juggling act in order to accommodate the various land use demands made upon them; in the Peak District part of that problem has been neatly removed by the complete exclusion of this area. This is also obvious as the route drops down to cross the River Wye: there is a huge contrast here between the scarred landscapes – Tunstead Quarry in Great Rocks Dale is one of the largest in Europe – just outside the Park boundary, and the peace and beauty of Chee Dale.

There's more to picturesque Chee Dale than meets the eye: Tunstead Quarry is next door, and the site of Blackwell Halt – once the shortest railway platform in Britain – lurks beneath the trees!

3 Peak Forest to Hayfield

8.5 miles (13.7 km)

In total contrast to the early stages, the next section of the Pennine Bridleway leads across the edge of the desolate moorland of the Dark – or High – Peak. This horseshoe-shaped swathe of tough millstone grit (gritstone) and shale, averaging around 2,000 feet (600 metres) above sea level, lies around three sides of the limestone plateau of the gentler White Peak, and provides a totally different experience. This is something that makes the whole Pennine Bridleway so fascinating: however you decide to split the route, you can be sure that the landscape will be constantly changing. Today is no exception. Soon after leaving Peak Forest the transition from limestone to gritstone becomes clear, and the route thereafter is along the edge of the Dark Peak, characterised by blanket bog – the annual rainfall here is around 60 inches (1,524 mm) – and rolling heather moorland, gloriously purple in August. Today's section of the Pennine Bridleway follows the line of an old packhorse trail, the Packhorse Road, which ran from Tideswell via Peak Forest to Hayfield across Roych Clough; there is a Packhorse Inn at Hayfield. Hayfield is perhaps best known today as the gathering point for the famous mass trespass that made its way towards Kinder Scout in the spring of 1932.

Although Peak Forest is somewhat carved up by the A623, there's more to the village than initially meets the eye, and it has an interesting history. It was originally an administrative centre for the Royal Forest, an exclusive hunting ground of around 40 square miles in area, created in the 12th century. The unusually dedicated church of King Charles the Martyr **25** originated as a private chapel (built in 1657) for the second Countess of Devonshire; the present structure dates from the 19th century. Being on Crown land, the church here lay outside the boundaries of normal ecclesiastical laws and in the 18th century became a sort of 'Gretna Green' for runaway couples until an Act of Parliament in 1804 put an end to the practice.

To continue on the Pennine Bridleway, from the A623 crossing **A** proceed straight ahead up Church Lane, signed Perryfoot. There's a general store on the right, so stock up with provisions for the day. Although it is only 9 miles (14.5 km) to Hayfield, the route is so spectacular that most users will want to take their time and not rush things. Pass the Methodist church on the left

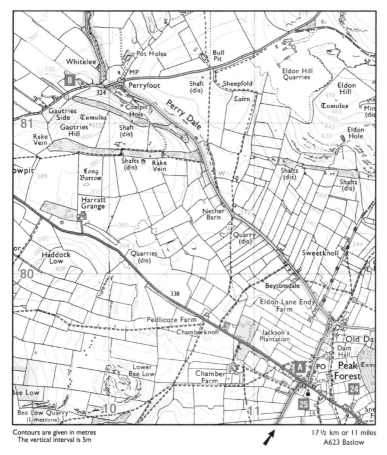

Contours are given in metres
The vertical interval is 5m

17½ km or 11 miles
A623 Baslow

– the Peak District has a long history of non-Conformism – and follow the lane as it bears left at Old Dam. This quiet lane runs between limestone-walled fields to pass a farm on the right, and through a gate by a cattle grid, and on through Perry Dale. Pass modern farm buildings on the left, go through a field gate by a cattle grid, and continue to a T-junction of lanes at Perryfoot. Turn left, then first right **B** on a narrow tarmac lane with a pond on the corner.

This is where you really start to notice a change in your surroundings, as underlying limestone gives way to gritstone. Keep an eye on the walls as you make your way up this quiet lane: pale, irregular-shaped limestone at the lower end gives way to dark, slabby, flattish gritstone as you gain height, and all around the fields are bigger, the hills in the distance higher and more open than anything encountered on the Pennine Bridleway so far. The lane veers left and then rises steeply uphill to pass Rushop Hall on the right. As it levels off look ahead onto the moorland to spot a rather incongruous rectangular structure. This is an air shaft for the Cowburn Tunnel **26** through the bulk of Colborne, carrying the railway line from Edale to Chapel-en-le-Frith and beyond. Don't be surprised if you hear a train whistle when you reach Roych Clough: the railway line emerges from the tunnel $1/2$ mile (0.8 km) to the south.

The lane soon meets the A625 Sheffield Road; cross over carefully **C** and go through a bridlegate on the other side. Immediately there are fabulous views ahead towards the steep-sided outline of South Head (1,621 feet/494 metres), with extraordinary parallel gritstone walls running right over the top and down the other side – the Pennine Bridleway passes just to the right of this easily recognised feature. The next part of the route, towards and through steep-sided Roych Clough, was at one time damaged and deeply rutted as a result of use by 4WD vehicles and insufficient maintenance. A huge amount of time and effort has been put into restoring the track and improving drainage to render it usable by walkers, cyclists and horse-riders, and it has really paid off: this is one of the most inspiring sections of the Pennine Bridleway in terms of landscape. Users should be aware, though, that 4WD vehicles and motorcycles have the right to use the first $2^{1}/_{4}$ miles (3.6 km) of the track, from the Sheffield Road as far as the top of Beet Lane. Along this section trail users should look out for specially designed lengths of alternative path running within the walls, parallel to and above the main track. The purpose of these paths is to offer a horse- and walker-friendly alternative to the more sunken, stony sections of track enjoyed by the vehicle users and technical mountain bikers.

Follow the track as it undulates along the moorland edge. Drop down to cross a stream, then follow the track uphill. It passes through a bridlegate, runs along the moorland edge, and through another gate, with a hay meadow on the right: such traditional hay meadows in the Dark Peak hold populations of curlew. At the end of the meadow pass through a field gate by a beech and sycamore plantation on the left. The track drops downhill to pass round the top of Bolehill Clough. Throughout the South Pennines these deep, steep-sided stream valleys are known as cloughs. As the landscape changes, so does local terminology: the dales of the White Peak have already been left far behind.

Continue on to pass wooded Green Low above the track on the right, and then pass through a field gate by a sycamore plantation on the right. As you drop steeply downhill between walls into Roych Clough – negotiating another field gate en route – look right to see the rolling heights of Brown Knoll (1,867 feet/569 metres) **27** and Horsehill Tor (1,765 feet/538 metres) **28**, rising to left and right above the head of Roych Clough.

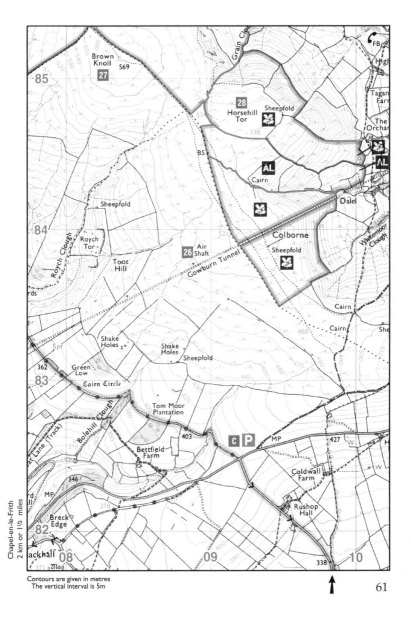

Contours are given in metres
The vertical interval is 5m

Notice how the restored track here is made up of stone, pitched and designed specifically to accommodate horse use as well as to stand up to vehicles. Roych Clough is a delightful spot, with scattered deciduous trees near the stream and glorious views up the clough towards Brown Knoll. Much of the Dark Peak is covered in blanket bog, believed to originate around 7,000 years ago, when Neolithic peoples started clearing trees from the area. The exposed soil became waterlogged; the consequent slow decay of mosses and plants has produced vast areas of peat bog. This unique habitat supports a great variety of specialised birds, plants and insects, and the area between Brown Knoll and towards the Kinder massif beyond holds one of the highest populations of nesting golden plover in the Peak District. The heather moorland results from management by local landowners in the past to create a habitat for the red grouse, mainstay of wealthy shooting estates in the 19th century. Areas of blackened ground can be seen at certain times of year; controlled burning encourages the growth of various plants, and grouse feed on the young heather shoots. The black grouse became extinct in the Peak District in the late 1990s.

The track crosses two fords in Roych Clough, then rises steeply uphill, parallel to a wall on the left, and past a ruined building. Continue along the edge of open moorland, through a field gate, then between walls. An uphill, stony stretch levels off a little by an overgrown pond on the left – users are asked to avoid disturbing breeding frogs! Just past this, walled Beet Lane runs off left (the end of the road for 4WD vehicles).

Proceed straight ahead between high walls, passing through a metal gate to enter the National Trust land at South Head, with a notice welcoming users to the High Peak. The track continues to pass beneath the right-hand slopes of South Head, and drops downhill – and this is where you just have to say 'Wow!' Pause for a breather and enjoy the most amazing views over the Kinder plateau. The track continues on, bearing left to pass between stone gateposts and then the slopes of South Head on the left, and the quaintly named Mount Famine **29**, rising to 1,552 feet (473 metres) on the right. The views now have changed completely – the town of Chapel-en-le-Frith ('Chapel-in-the-Forest') can be seen in the valley below. Pass through a metal gate to leave National Trust land. The track, now earthy, runs across an open grassy area with beautiful views left across to steep-sided Chinley Churn, rising to 1,480 feet (451 metres) beyond the Hayfield Road on the opposite side of the valley.

Continue on through two field gates (at right angles) and almost immediately pass through a small field gate next to a field gate onto a walled track, dropping downhill. This joins another gritty track; bear right downhill between walls. You get the feeling that you're returning to civilisation: you can hear the buzz of traffic on the A624 in the valley below left. Where the track bends sharp left, and a green lane goes straight on, turn right **D** along a narrow fenced track with a wall left and stock fence right. Go through a gate into a field, keeping the wall on the left, and pass through a gate in the wall straight ahead to be rewarded with more fantastic views over the Kinder massif.

Bear left, downhill, across the scarp slope; this is a delightful path, with great views over the River Sett in Coldwell Clough **30** below right – a really lovely, easy finish to the day. The path then

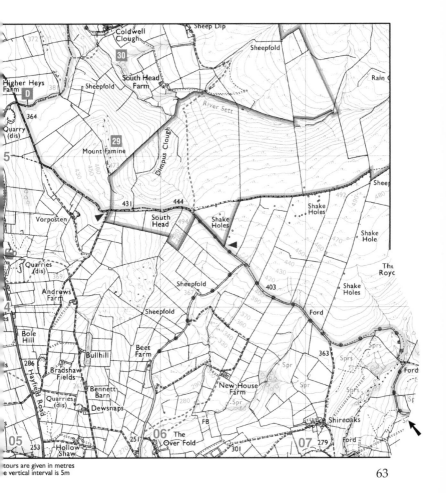

tours are given in metres
e vertical interval is 5m

drops downhill to hit a lane. Turn left and follow the lane for 100 yards/metres, before turning left uphill off the lane on a path that runs across the contours past scattered hawthorns to reach a gate at the edge of Elle Bank coniferous plantation. There are wide views here over Tunstead Clough Farm; Kinder Reservoir lies in the next fold of hills beyond. Pass through the gate and keep straight on, with the wall left, along the edge of the plantation; steep bracken-covered slopes drop away right. As the path rounds the hill it becomes walled, with good views over the campsite by the River Sett below, and the steep, wooded slopes of Kinder Bank **31** beyond. The path continues to drop downhill, passing a field on the right before entering mixed deciduous woodland.

Pass through a bridlegate, with a bridge over the River Sett right. Keep straight on along a gravelly track, with the river on the right. The track becomes tarmac, and runs into tarmac Valley Road; keep straight ahead – the river is now below right. Pass terraced houses to meet Highgate Road; turn right down-hill for 10 yards/metres to a T-junction; turn right **E** down Church Street in the middle of Hayfield, once within the Royal Forest, now an attractive village with cafés, tearooms and three-storey weavers' cottages.

Hayfield lies on the course of the old Roman road from Buxton to Glossop, and was the focus of several packhorse trails in medieval times, including one that ran along the Sett Valley and

Peaceful Hayfield once played an important part in the history of 'the right to roam'.

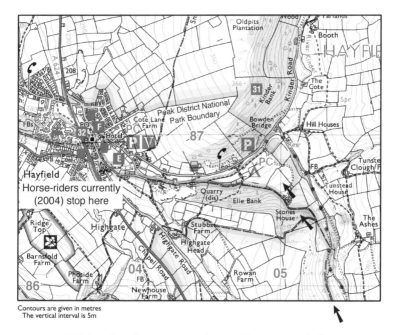

Contours are given in metres
The vertical interval is 5m

over to Edale. Another ran north to Glossop and then on to Holmfirth, where wool from Hayfield was taken to be dyed. In the early 18th century the village developed around the textile industry; the fast-flowing waters of the Sett and Kinder rivers rendered Hayfield ideal for industrial development, and millowners from Manchester turned their attention to this quiet community, at that time reliant on farming, and home spinning and weaving. By 1860 the valley was dotted with spinning and calico-printing mills, and Hayfield prospered. As well as aiding Hayfield's industrial development, the coming of the railway from Manchester along the Sett Valley in 1868 also opened the village up to the early 'tourist' trade: a trip to Hayfield – the start of open country – provided a much-needed break for thousands of millworkers from the city.

Pass The George Hotel (circa 1575) on the left, and turn left **F** just before St Matthews Church **32** (built in 1818 on the site of an older church that was destroyed by floodwater), following signs for the Sett Valley Trail, car park, toilets and bus station. This narrow lane leads to a Pegasus crossing over the busy A624 – built in 1978 to bypass the centre of the village – into the car park, situated on the site of the former station yard at the terminus of the Sett Valley railway line. There are separate horsebox- and car-parking areas here (charges apply), as well as a hitching rail and tap, information centre toilets, picnic area and cycle-hire facilities.

A wonderful springtime view from the Pennine Bridleway over the Sett Valley and the west

The right to roam

The views over the Kinder plateau from South Head are quite fantastic, and it becomes instantly clear why Kinder Scout – which rises to 2,074 feet (632 metres), the highest point in the Peak District National Park – has played such an important role in the history of 'the right to roam'. No one could fail to be moved by such a view, and be drawn to further exploration. In the late 19th century rambling clubs were set up in the north of England, and the activity increased in popularity in the early years of the 20th century. From the late 1890s, too, the early climbers were turning their attention towards the gritstone edges of the Dark Peak, and the moorland was attracting the 'bog trotters', who concentrated on traversing difficult patches of terrain at speed. This all gave strength to the campaign for public access in the Peak District – it is thought that by the early 1930s, at weekends during the summer, as many as 10,000 ramblers could be found in the area – and the first 'mass trespass' took place on 24 April 1932. Around 500 walkers assembled in Hayfield and set off into the hills in peace-

...pes of the Kinder plateau.

ful protest concerning lack of access to the countryside. They were turned back by a group of gamekeepers, and five of their number were imprisoned, but the event raised the profile of the whole issue and contributed towards the eventual passing of the National Parks and Access to the Countryside Act in 1949.

It is also fitting that Britain's first and toughest long-distance footpath, the Pennine Way – opened in 1965 and now designated as a National Trail – should have its southern end in the Dark Peak. This 268-mile (431-km) route follows the backbone of England from Edale, south-east of Kinder Scout, to Kirk Yetholm, just over the Scottish Border. The first chunk of the route, over the demanding Kinder plateau, provides an early test for walkers, particularly in bad weather. The idea for such a route was first mooted as long ago as 1935 by Tom Stephenson, a walker and journalist, and on a couple of occasions further north the Pennine Bridleway and Pennine Way touch each other, if briefly.

4 Hayfield to Uppermill

Walkers' route 19 miles (30.6 km)
Cyclists' route 20.5 miles (33 km)
Horse-riders' route (from Torside – see below) 12.1 miles (19.4 km)

It has to be said that today's route starts and ends with a bang but – temporarily – suffers something of a setback for a short distance in the middle. The problems of devising a long-distance route that is suitable for three different groups of user are many, and this section highlights that fact: it has not yet been possible to finalise the National Trail route through the Glossop area between Monk's Road and Bottoms Reservoir. Whilst ultimately the aim is to provide a single, attractive route for horses, bikes and walkers by 2006, for the time being interim routes are suggested for each user type. *For an overview of the routes for different users on this section of the bridleway, see insert on Key Map 2, pages 10-11.* Any changes to the routes described below will be signed on the ground, with further details available on the website www.nationaltrail.co.uk/penninebridleway.

Horse-riders: Hayfield to Bottoms Reservoir
It is recommended that horse-riders break their journey at Hayfield and box to Torside car park, from where they can follow the lovely Longdendale Trail (part of the Trans Pennine Trail) back towards Glossop to rejoin the Pennine Bridleway at Bottoms Reservoir. Whilst it is possible to use public bridleway and road to access the Trans Pennine Trail at Gamesley and follow this to Bottoms Reservoir – so avoiding the need to box – the roads are twisting, and the traffic often fast moving.

CYCLISTS' AND WALKERS' ROUTE FROM HAYFIELD TO COWN EDGE

The route through the outskirts of Glossop leaves a lot to be desired in terms of landscape quality, but it doesn't last long, and the superb countryside traversed before and after more than makes up for it. Again, make sure that you stock up with provisions before leaving Hayfield.

After crossing the A624 in Hayfield **A**, the Bridleway continues straight ahead along the right-hand edge of the bus-turning area and then along the right edge of a small area of woodland, before merging with the Sett Valley Trail. This 2 $^1/_2$-mile (4-km) trail for walkers, cyclists and horse-riders runs from the old station area at Hayfield to New Mills, along the course of the old single-track railway. The railway was constructed in 1868 to bring raw materials to Hayfield's mills and to transport finished products away. It finally closed in 1970, opening as a trail in 1979.

As might be expected, the bridleway along the old line is level, straight and even. If you're on the trail in May, you'll come across Bluebell Wood on the right just after the first gate – a glorious sight. Pass a small reservoir on the right, and follow the trail as it bears left towards a road (leaving the line of the railway), then turns right downhill alongside the road (this is a steep descent: cyclists are asked to dismount). The trail bears left to pass through a gate onto the road. The Sett Valley Trail continues over the road, but the Pennine Bridleway turns right down Station Road, passing a small café on the left and crossing the River Sett. Just past a very gracious terrace of cottages – The Crescent – on the right, turn right **B** up a steep, walled, stone-setted way that rises up behind the cottages beneath big beech trees. This becomes an earthy path, and levels off to meet a gate, leading onto a lane on a U-bend. Keep straight on uphill, along a rough tarmac lane, climbing gently all the time. Cross the next lane, opposite terraced cottages, and continue uphill on a lane to the right of the cottages.

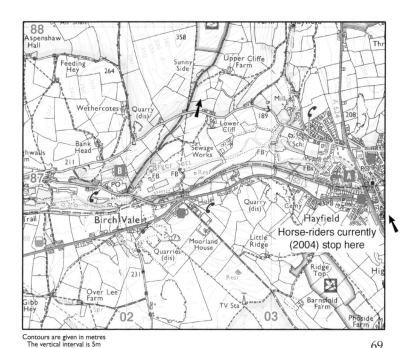

Contours are given in metres
The vertical interval is 5m

There now follows a long, steep climb to the National Trust's Lantern Pike **33**, which rises to 1,224 feet (373 metres). (Cyclists – on foot – and walkers would be well advised to make a quick detour up to the summit, where there are fantastic views over the Kinder massif to the east and Greater Manchester to the west.) The views right over Hayfield, cradled within green hills with the high moorland of the Dark Peak rising beyond, are fabulous. Follow the tarmac lane steeply uphill, eventually passing a remote house – Sunny Side – on the left, at which point the tarmac ends and the track becomes rough. Where the track levels and forks keep left and continue to a gate, following the track through rough grassland and heather around the contours of Lantern Pike, with a wall on the right. The views east over Little Hayfield in the valley, and the lofty Kinder plateau beyond, are superb. Descend to pass through a gate to leave National Trust land; the track enters a field and becomes indistinct. Head diagonally left, aiming for the far corner of the field where two gates can be seen. Turn left through the bridlegate by a five-bar gate in the corner of the field onto a track leading to Blackshaw Farm on the right.

Continue along the walled track. Almost immediately there are great views ahead of flat-topped, craggy Cown Edge Rocks **34** (the walkers' route runs along the top of this classic gritstone feature). The track continues, keeping Matleymoor Farm and pond on the right. Continue along the track until you pass through a metal field gate, leading onto a wide, walled, stone track. Turn left, downhill, to meet a quiet tarmac lane. Turn right uphill **C**, following the lane right, then sharp left before levelling off. Pass Butcher's Piece Farm on the left; the lane bends sharp right towards Monk's Road **D**.

At this point turn left and follow the lane through a gate marked Cown Edge Farm. Continue along the lane through rough grassland; the lane bears left towards the farm. There's a very remote, slightly desolate feel around here. Keep going straight ahead up a deeply rutted, rocky, banked and fenced track. This runs over a saddle **E** in the Cown Edge ridge.

Cyclists and walkers now take different routes, meeting again at Lees Hill, north-west of Tintwistle. The two routes actually cross each other south-west of Glossop – a prosperous textile town in times past. In 1831 it was said that Glossop had 56 mills – mainly cotton – out of a total of 112 in the whole of Derbyshire. The rather unusual name derives from the Anglo-Saxon 'Glott's valley' or 'Glott's Hop' – hence 'Glossop'.

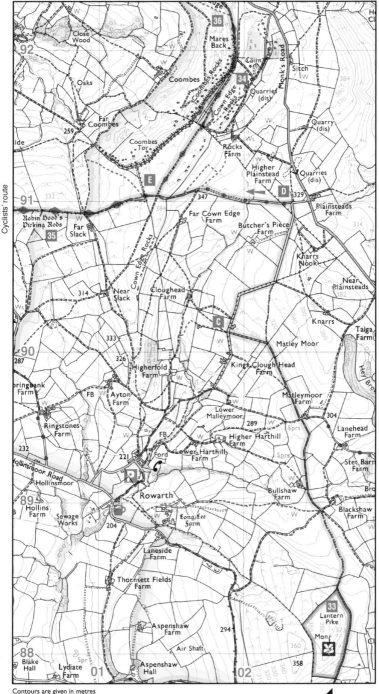

Cyclists' route

Contours are given in metres
The vertical interval is 5m

CYCLISTS' ROUTE FROM COWN EDGE TO BOTTOMS RESERVOIR

Cyclists can now can enjoy a long downhill section to Charlesworth, far below in the Etherow Valley. Keep straight on over the saddle **E**, with views over Greater Manchester ahead. Pass through a small metal gate and follow the fenced path left, then right. The narrow, uneven path runs downhill and through a gate, with the house at Far Slack left. Continue downhill on the edge of cattle pasture – the track tends to be muddy – with the wall left. Pass through a metal gate and continue downhill past stone blocks – 'Robin Hood's Picking Rods' **35** – on the left. Once known as the Maiden Stones, legend has it that a Druidic sacrifice took place here in the 1st century AD, in the hope of deterring the Roman advance – but to no avail! It is also claimed that the blocks were later used by Robin Hood for stringing his bows and for target practice. The track improves and becomes broader. Continue downhill and through another gate; keep on to meet the track leading right to Moorside. Bear left downhill to meet tarmac Gun Road; turn right downhill **F**. Here the interim route joins the Pennine Cycleway NCN Route 68; cyclists should follow the cycleway signs to meet the Longdendale Trail at Bottoms Reservoir. There now follows a lovely downhill run of about 1 1/4 miles (2 km) to the Glossop Road, but take care: the lane is at times narrow, and there are some blind corners. At the T-junction

Cyclists on the trail north of Lantern Pike, looking towards Cown Edge.

by the kennels turn right downhill, and follow this twisting lane down New Mills Road to meet the Glossop Road at Holehouse. Turn right **G**. This is a busy road, and cyclists can't escape from it for just under 1 1/2 miles (2.4 km). Keep straight on, eventually climbing uphill to the junction of roads in Charlesworth – where there are a couple of pubs, and shops for provisions – and continue ahead, eventually crossing the Manchester–Glossop railway line on wide Glossop Bridge, just south of Gamesley.

Walkers' route

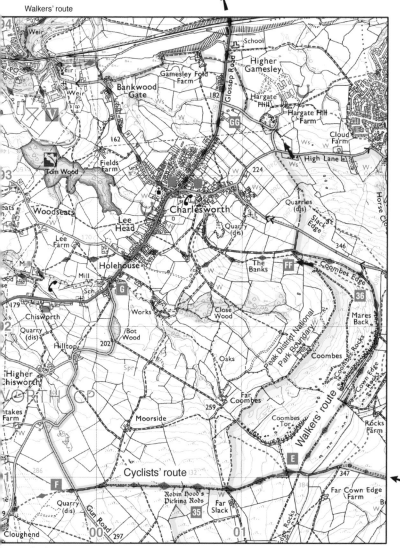

The Glossop road bears right once over the railway line; ignore any signs left immediately over the bridge. About 20 yards/metres further on turn left **H** between terraced houses, also signed Trans Pennine Trail (a coast-to-coast route for walkers and cyclists – and in some places horse-riders – linking the Mersey to the Humber). Continue across a grassy area to meet a road on the edge of a housing estate. Turn left and follow this for about 1 mile (1.6 km). This isn't the most attractive part of the route, but cyclists should be able to move through it pretty swiftly! Pass the earthworks of Melandra Roman fort **37** on the left. Situated at the entrance to Longdendale, the original wooden fort was constructed around AD 75 and rebuilt in stone in the early 2nd century. A civil settlement (*vicus*) grew up around it; before the Gamesley estate was built, excavations revealed various buildings, including a bathhouse. It is thought that the fort was demolished by the Romans when they pulled out of the area in the mid 2nd century.

Where the road bends sharp right, and there is a road sign for Melandra Castle Road on the edge of a broad grassy area on the left, turn left **I** on (unsigned) Cottage Lane, passing between red-brick houses on the right, and a small parking area on the left. After about 100 yards/metres this tarmac lane becomes very rough; turn left to leave it along a sandy and initially railed path. This broad, level path eventually passes along the other side of the Roman fort. Where the path divides, take the right fork, which drops downhill to cross a tarmac lane. Turn right to cross Glossop Brook on a railed bridge. The tarmac path turns left, then bears right along the River Etherow (on the left). Pass through a kissing-gate to meet the A57.

Cross over via the Pegasus crossing and go through a gate on the other side. Follow the path uphill, with modern houses on the right; the path levels and passes through a grassy area before narrowing to descend between industrial buildings on the left and the backs of houses on the right. Pass through a gate to meet busy Woolley Bridge Road on the edge of Hadfield. Turn right **J**; after 50 yards/metres take the left fork. Follow this road past industrial buildings, and St Charles Church **38** on the right, uphill to a crossroads, with The New Lamp pub on the corner. Turn left downhill, signed Tintwistle. Just before Tintwistle Bridge (which crosses the River Etherow as it emerges from Longdendale) turn right **K** along Goddard Lane. Around 50 yards/metres along the lane bear left through water corporation pillars. Follow the broad path towards the dam of Bottoms

Reservoir, the lowest in the chain of Longdendale reservoirs, constructed in the mid 19th century and, at the time, the largest artificial expanse of water in the world. Follow the path as it bears left to run below the dam, and then right uphill on the other side. Pass through gateposts onto a tarmac way, and follow signs to the crossing of the A628 (an old turnpike road from Cheshire to Yorkshire, dating from 1731).

Contours are given in metres
The vertical interval is 5m

CYCLISTS' AND HORSE-RIDERS' ROUTE FROM BOTTOMS RESERVOIR TO LEES HILL

Horse-riders rejoin the Pennine Bridleway south of the A628 crossing, via the Longdendale Trail (see page 68) from Torside car park. This lovely route runs along the edges of Torside, Rhodeswood and Valehouse Reservoirs before bearing north-west to reach the A628 north of Bottoms Reservoir. A Pegasus crossing is due to be installed here in 2004; until this is in operation, cross with care. Horse-riders are advised that there are a great many HGVs using this busy road.

From the crossing, cyclists and horse-riders should continue straight up short but steep stone-setted Chapel Brow to a T-junction in Tintwistle village; turn left. (The route will eventually continue further east before turning north, so watch out for signs here.) Tintwistle (quaintly pronounced 'Tinsel') was mentioned in the Domesday Book of 1086, and had an incredible 11 pubs in 1851! Pass The Bull's Head **39** on the left – a good place for a break if cyclists need to recover from the dreary stretch just completed – and continue into the village centre, with a war memorial on the left. Just before the lane ahead descends to the A628, turn right **L** along stone-setted Arnfield Lane.

All at once the traffic, noise and industrial feel of the Etherow Valley is left far behind – cyclists will experience a great sense of relief at being back out in the countryside again. Views open up over Arnfield Reservoir to the left, and towards Hollingworth Moor ahead left, with the steep scarp of Lees Hill at the moor's northern end – walkers rejoin the main Pennine Bridleway at the base of Lees Hill. Keep straight on along the lane, which becomes tarmac and drops steeply downhill to cross Arnfield Brook, then rises up the other side of the clough.

Where you see 'Private: No Entry' signs ahead, turn sharp right **M** to leave the lane up a gritty, sandy track. Pass sycamore and beech trees below right, then pass through a bridlegate by a five-bar gate. Follow the walled track uphill. Pass through another bridlegate, and continue climbing relentlessly uphill; all but the toughest cyclists will be forced to dismount and push their bikes. Where another track goes straight ahead towards a coniferous plantation on the edge of Arnfield Moor, bear left on the track, following a wall on the left. Horse-riders and cyclists are requested to keep to the track and not be tempted to stray onto open ground. Lees Hill, rising to 1,173 feet (357 metres), is in clear view ahead. Follow this lovely,

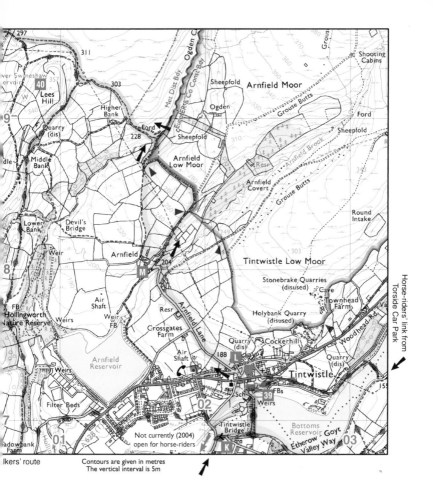

Walkers' route

Contours are given in metres
The vertical interval is 5m

grassy track as it runs along the edge of heather and grass
moorland before dropping via a gate into steep-sided Ogden
Clough, a very pretty spot and particularly lovely in August,
when the slopes are clothed with purple heather. Cross Ogden
Brook on a low stone bridge, suitable for horse use (horses can
also use the ford), leaving the Peak District National Park for
the last time and crossing the border into Tameside.

Follow the track as it runs along the edge of the moor, with
a wall on the left. Breeding waders – lapwing, curlew, snipe
and redshank – may be seen on the wet fields (known as
flushes) along these moorland edges, where excess water seeps
out from under the blanket bog. Pass through a bridlegate and
follow the wall as it bears left under pylons to meet a stile in
the fence ahead at the base of Lees Hill **40**.

77

Walkers' route
from Cown Edge to Lees Hill

From the saddle **E** turn right over a stile onto rough grassland. Walk straight ahead, eventually crossing a stile in a gritstone wall just above craggy Cown Edge Rocks (right), with fantastic views. Pass a spruce plantation on the left; beyond the end of it pass through a broken-down wall. Views (left) open up over the sweep of Coombes Edge **36** as it curves towards Charlesworth; ahead right is another coniferous plantation. Just before the next wall (coming in right) turn left over a stile, then immediately right along the edge of Coombes Rocks, with a wire fence right. At the time of the Roman invasion this was thought to be the site of a battle between the advancing Romans and local tribesmen, who were crushed: beware ghostly warriors if you're up here on a moonlit night . . . This narrow path runs along the edge of the ridge, with a steep drop over the crags left: it's a spectacular spot. Follow the edge of the ridge as it curves left, walking slightly downhill across grassland; Monks Road, which goes to Hayfield, comes into view right. The open grassland ends at a group of livestock pens; keep straight on over four stiles to a gritty track by a cattle grid. Turn right **FF** along the track to meet Monks Road.

Cross the road and over a small stile left of a five-bar gate. There is no visible path across this field, so keep straight ahead, bearing slightly left, always downhill. Where an area of old workings suddenly appears below right, look left to find a stile in the stock fence along the bottom of the field: rugby goalposts in the valley below should be in direct line with this. Cross the stile and keep straight on down the next field, bearing slightly right at the end over a stile onto High Lane. Cross over and down narrow Hargate Hill Lane, bearing sharp left downhill at Wayside House, then sharp right.

The lane levels off; turn right over a stile **GG** and go through the rugby club car park. Pass behind the club house; turn right over a stile, then left along the field edge. Go over the stile in the next fence, and straight ahead along the left edge of the next field, with a wire fence left. Pass through a kissing-gate at the end of the field, onto the drive leading to the equestrian centre. Keep straight ahead, to the right of the pond, to meet the Glossop Road.

Cross directly over the A626 and follow the field-edge footpath to Gamesley Ford Farm. On approaching the farm, turn right along the track, then left through a set of gates. At the end of the next field, follow the path left along the fence and down into a

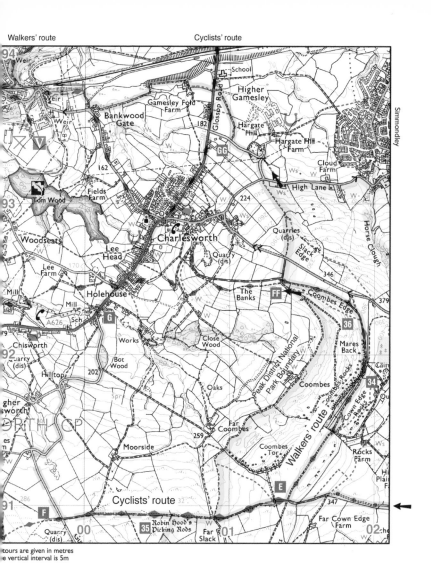

tours are given in metres
e vertical interval is 5m

woodland, then over a bridge. The path emerges into another field at the top. Follow the right side of the fields, close to the woodland, dipping back down to a stream and up again towards some farm buildings on the horizon. Go over the stile to the right of the buildings onto a track, which leads to the road.

Do not cross the road; turn sharp right along a track (on the Trans Pennine Trail: see page 103). Follow this to Broadbottom, meeting the road under the railway viaduct. Continue over the river bridge and through Broadbottom village. Go under the next railway bridge and right onto Hague Road; follow this past some large houses for about ¹/₂ mile (0.8 km). At the house called The Hague fork right (Valley Way) and follow the track for another ¹/₂ mile (0.8 km) to a farm. Just after the farm, follow a path to the left behind buildings, then turn right and join another track to Pear Tree Farm. Pass to the left of the farm, following Valley Way signs along a sunken track and across fields to the bottom of a hill. Cross a small bridge and go straight along a fenced track. After two more fields a gate to the right of conifers leads through a farmyard to a hidden stile to the right of a gate on the bridge. From here follow the track for a short way to the A57.

Cross the road onto Junction Road/Woolley Close. Turn right onto the Boulevard, and go directly though some gates into Woolley Bridge Copse. Keep going through the wood to another gate that leads onto Water Lane. Turn left, and follow the lane to the busy A628 where there is a pedestrian crossing.

Walkers' route

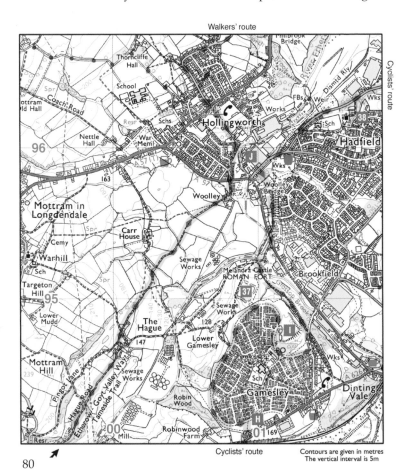

Cyclists' route

Contours are given in metres
The vertical interval is 5m

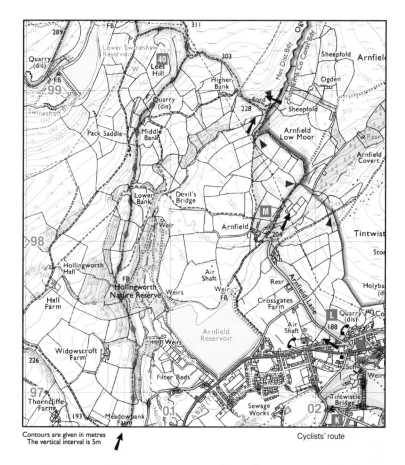

Contours are given in metres
The vertical interval is 5m

Cyclists' route

Cross over; follow Green Lane through Hollingworth village to reach Meadow Bank Farm at the end of the built-up area. Take the footpath left near the entrance to the farm (not Cow Lane). Follow this along the upper side of farm buildings, then turn right to a stile in the field corner. Follow the path on the right-hand side of the next field before descending into a wooded area and over a stream. The path crosses two more fields, intersected by large trees, before reaching a kissing-gate into Hollingworth Nature Reserve. Once through the reserve the path follows the field edges, with the line of old hedgerow and walls on the left.

Pass through a gate below a coniferous plantation and follow a grassy track to the next footpath junction. Cross the stony track to a stile and continue on a walled grassy track. Where it ends (with Lees Hill rising left) cross the narrow stile to the right to join the main Pennine Bridleway opposite a pylon, and turn left.

ROUTE FOR ALL USERS FROM LEES HILL TO UPPERMILL

Walkers join the bridleway over the stile ahead, and turn left. Those already on the bridleway should not cross the stile, but bear right, keeping the wall on the left, along a broad, grassy track. Pass through a bridlegate and descend gently towards the dam of Higher Swineshaw Reservoir. Go through a bridle-gate, bearing right to cross the dam through another gate.

For the next section (through Brushes Valley), trail users should note that on rare occasions during the shooting season they may be asked to wait for a few minutes while a shooting party passes through. Your co-operation with any such request would be appreciated; this was one of the management mea-sures agreed with the estate representatives in granting a new right of access along this track for cyclists and horse-riders.

Turn left on the other side of the dam on a quiet tarmac lane, descending gently for about 1 mile (1.6 km) to Walkerwood Reservoir – a lovely run for cyclists. Pass Lower Swineshaw Reservoir (left), fringed by a pretty plantation of mixed decidu-ous trees. It's so quiet here you can easily lapse into daydream mode – so it comes as a shock when suddenly, as the lane curves right, you are confronted with a huge panoramic view over the urban sprawl of Greater Manchester! Civilisation is never very far away. The lane runs along the edge of Brushes Reservoir, past a house on the left, to reach a cross-tracks. A lane leads left down to the dam between Brushes and Walkerwood Reservoirs; tarmac Brushes Lane keeps straight ahead.

Turn right **N** through a gate, on a narrow tarmac lane, rising uphill. After about 200 yards/metres the tarmac lane bends sharp right and becomes rough; keep straight ahead on a rough track to pass through a bridlegate. Follow the now grassy, undu-lating track around the edge of Harridge Pike, with views over Millbrook left. Pass through a bridlegate and continue to meet a tarmac lane between Copper Farm and Higher Hyde Green; keep ahead, slightly uphill. Pass through the houses at Higher Hyde Green; where the tarmac ends keep ahead on a rough track, which runs uphill to pass derelict cottages on the left. There are good views ahead over Buckden Moor and the great scar of Buckden Vale Quarry **41**. The track becomes rocky and bumpy before descending past a cream-coloured cottage on the left, at which point the surface improves. Follow the track down-hill into the valley to reach the edge of a new housing estate on the outskirts of Carrbrook, in the shadow of the quarry. Bear left and then right on a lane around the edge of the estate, passing Woodview, part of Stalybridge Country Park, on the left. At the small crossroads by the entrance to the estate – Stonemead – keep straight on along the tarmac lane. Follow the lane as it bears left over a stream, passing another part of the country park – Cowbury Green – on the right. Keep ahead on Castle Lane; pass between terraced houses, at the end of which bear right on a bridleway that runs parallel with the road, uphill.

The bridleway bends right for a few yards alongside a lane that runs right up to the quarry, and passes through a gate. Cross the lane to the quarry and take the track **O** which runs straight ahead around the contours of the hill; note that there is a lot of

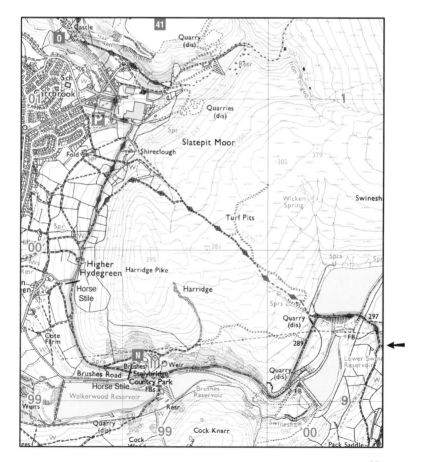

old farm machinery hereabouts. The broad, gritty track – Moor Edge Road – is quite rough in places, and continues on to cross a concrete road. Follow the track as it dips down to cross a stream, then rises again and continues along the contours. The track joins another, leading to a cottage above right; keep straight on. Almost immediately the track splits; take the right fork uphill, to round the edge of Noonsun Hill. Uppermill, the end of today's route, can be seen in the Tame Valley ahead. This part of the western Pennines, around the upper reaches of the Tame and its tributaries, and straddling the Lancashire/Yorkshire border, is the ancient parish of Saddleworth. These river valleys at one time supported a great number of textile mills; Gatehead Mill, the first cotton mill in Saddleworth, was built in 1781. One of the last woollen mills in the area, Buckley New Mill in Uppermill, built in the mid 19th century, finally closed its doors as recently as 1979.

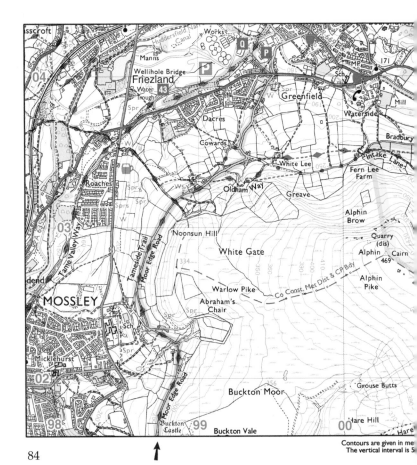

Contours are given in me
The vertical interval is 5

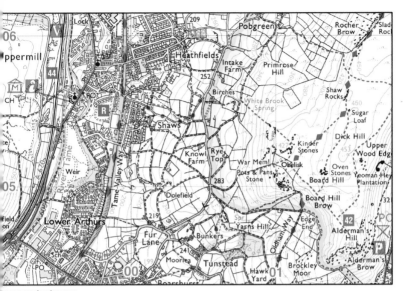

ntours are given in metres
he vertical interval is 5m

Eventually the track becomes tarmac; look straight ahead over Greenfield, in the valley of the Chew Brook, for fabulous views of Alderman's Hill **42**, with its fine obelisk war memorial (1923), and the crags of Alderman's Brow overlooking Dovestone Reservoir (completed 1967), which lies far below. The great bulk of Saddleworth Moor rises in the distance, haunt of the peregrine falcon and the shy migrant ring ouzel, moorland equivalent of the blackbird, an early spring arrival. The lane (known as Lane Head) descends steeply to cross a stream under sycamores, then bears left downhill, passing Intake Lane on the right (line of an old steam tramway that was used during the construction of Chew Reservoir in 1914). Keep ahead downhill through farmland and then houses as the edge of Greenfield is reached via Friezland Lane.

The lane meets the busy A635 Manchester Road; turn left for a few yards and then cross over and down Station Lane (access only) – Greenfield largely developed with the coming of the railway along the Tame Valley in 1850 and the building of cotton mills in the Chew Brook Valley. The lane ends at the gates to Station House; bear right through a gate for 50 yards/metres to meet the Tame Valley Way, part of which runs along the old railway trackbed. NB: The facilities at Friezland **43** may be found along the trail $3/4$ mile/1.2 km to the left here, and include horsebox parking, a water trough, mounting ramp and an outdoor ménage.

Turn right **Q** and follow the smooth-surfaced trail through mixed woodland; it soon drops downhill and bears left to cross Chew Brook, the outflow from Dovestone Reservoir. The Pennine Bridleway then passes through a parking area with the squash club on the left. Cross a minor road and keep ahead on a path uphill through a grassy area; pass through staggered barriers to cross the A669 Chew Valley Road. The path continues over a grassy area to reach the corner of Higher Arthurs, with a lane leading off right; turn left and then immediately right along Carr Lane. About 10 yards/metres later turn right through bollards to return to the old railway trackbed. The next section is very straight, level and dull; where it narrows with high fences on the left horses are asked to walk; cyclists should slow down. The track passes under a tunnel; keep straight ahead as the track becomes tarmac and passes the swimming pool and all-weather football pitch on the left. When the swimming pool car park is reached **R**, note signs left off the trail to the centre of Uppermill **44**. Even if you don't plan to overnight here, take some time for an exploration of Uppermill, a 'new' industrial village in the late 18th century, now a pleasant town with terraced weavers' cottages, cafes and galleries. Saddleworth Museum, in the High Street, is a fund of useful information on the area.

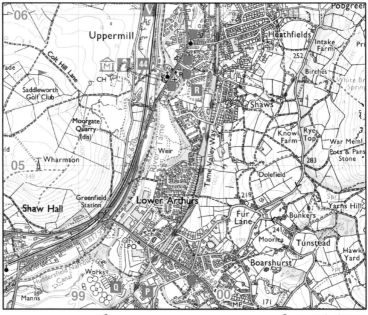

Contours are given in metres
The vertical interval is 5m

The Longdendale Valley Reservoirs

Although by the time you've reached the dam at Bottoms Reservoir all you really want to do is breathe a sigh of relief and push on back into open countryside again, it's worth pausing to think about the fascinating history of Longdendale.

Look back towards the dam of Bottoms Reservoir from the A628 crossing in Tintwistle and you will notice the close juxtaposition of reservoir and industry in the valley. During the late 18th century there was rapid industrial development along the Etherow Valley, with small water-powered mills being superseded by all kinds of industrial buildings; by the mid 19th century the area was reliant on the production of cotton goods. Five main reservoirs were built in Longdendale from 1848 to 1877 in response to demands for a fresh water supply for the rapidly increasing population of Manchester and Salford; two smaller ones, Hollingworth and Arnside, supplemented those in the main valley. The lower two – Bottoms and Valehouse (named after the mills that lie beneath their waters) – were constructed to supply compensation water for the River Etherow, a tributary of the Mersey. Wealthy millowners objected to the proposals, concerned that water supplies to their mills along the Etherow would be disrupted. They demanded that a gauge be installed at Bottoms Reservoir, and during the late 19th century a millowner's representative met the reservoir keeper every day at 6am to check that the river was receiving the agreed amount of water. The catchment area of Longdendale – rising to 2,000 feet (610 metres) at Holme Moss – covers over 30 square miles, with an average annual rainfall of 52 $^1/_2$ inches (1,335 mm).

It was an enormous undertaking: over 1,000 navvies were employed at Bottoms, working mainly with hand tools and unsophisticated machinery. Hundreds more were employed further up the valley on construction of the 3-mile (4.8-km) Woodhead Tunnel, built 1838–45 to take the Manchester–Sheffield railway line under the Pennines. This, the first trans-Pennine route, was hugely expensive in terms of both money and lives, through a combination of accidents and disease, including a cholera outbreak in 1849. Many of the navvies and their families were buried at Woodhead Chapel, on the banks of the highest reservoir in Longdendale. The first tunnel was completed in 1845; a second in 1852. After years of fluctuating fortunes – and despite a new tunnel being opened in 1953, and the line being electrified – it was closed to passengers in 1970, and completely closed in 1981.

5 Uppermill to Summit

17 miles (27.4 km)

This section of the Pennine Bridleway is characterised by long climbs, and extraordinary contrasts between the bleak, remote moorland of the Pennine edge and fast-moving, somehow inappropriate A roads, which seem completely out of place after several days on the trail. The day starts with a steady uphill stretch out of the Tame Valley towards the bulk of Standedge, and then undulates across the bleak moorland, passing strings of reservoirs, before the final climb from Hollingworth Lake up onto Syke Moor. You are keenly aware of lines of communication on this stretch: many of the A roads to be crossed follow the lines of the old trans-Pennine packhorse trails and of later turnpike roads; and the magnificent yet intrusive M62 viaduct also has to be negotiated. A real sense of achievement is experienced on the final long, gentle, downhill stretch towards Summit and the link with the Mary Towneley Loop. On reaching the Loop users have a choice: this guidebook recommends tackling it in a clockwise direction, but it is extremely well waymarked and would be easy to follow either clockwise or anticlockwise.

From the swimming-pool car park **A**, the Pennine Bridleway continues along the old railway trackbed through the outskirts of Uppermill, almost immediately crossing a road on a bridge: horses are asked to walk. Proceed through a wooded section and over another road, eventually passing a school on the left. The trail drops left to leave the trackbed and follows a wide path to pass the school, before descending through an area of grassland and scattered trees. Continue uphill to pass through an open gateway and across a tarmac drive; keep ahead round a gate and climb steeply through a patch of woodland. Turn left for 20 yards/metres, then right **B**, passing the entrance to Ryefields Farm on the right. It's good to be back in rural surroundings again.

Follow this quiet, narrow lane. Where it bends 90 degrees right by three-storeyed cottages at Field Top, keep straight ahead up the track, passing Hollingreave Farm on the left. Pass through a five-bar gate onto a sandy fenced track, with good views over the upper Tame Valley. Keep straight ahead, passing a group of buildings on the left; bear right past the entrance to Holly Grove Farm on the left. Keep going uphill towards a red-brick bungalow. At the T-junction turn left downhill on Ward Lane, passing the bungalow on the right. Opposite a public footpath sign on

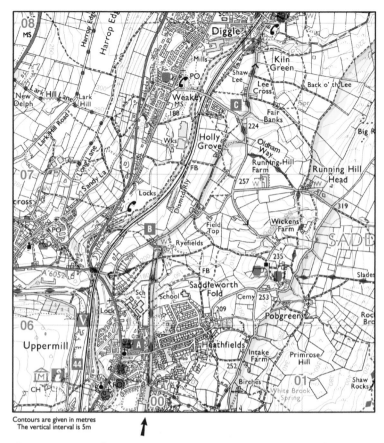

Contours are given in metres
The vertical interval is 5m

the left, bear right **C** at a triangular junction of lanes. Keep going steeply downhill, then uphill to level off at Lee Cross Farm. Drop downhill again to pass renovated mill buildings on the right; cross a stream, and Kiln Green church on the right, and follow the main lane (Lee Side) as it bears right uphill to cross Station Road at Diglea. Keep straight ahead to pass between the Diggle Hotel and its car park on a rough track – Boat Lane.

The 20-mile (32.2-km) Huddersfield Narrow Canal negotiated the bulk of moorland known as Standedge via the Standedge Tunnel, completed in 1811. Boat Lane is thought to have been the route along which the narrowboat horses were lead to re-join the canal on the far side of Standedge. There was no towpath through the Standedge Tunnel; the boats were 'legged' through by men lying on their backs, their feet braced against the tunnel wall. In the early 19th century it was recorded that this exercise could be completed in an amazing 1 hour 20 minutes, for the

Three-storeyed weavers' cottages, so characteristic of the South Pennines, at Diglea.

princely sum of 1/6d (7½p)! Today this is also the route of the Standedge Trail, a circular 10-mile (16-km) walking route that makes use of a number of old packhorse trails and turnpike roads. Follow Boat Lane past the entrance to the Standedge Railway tunnel below left **45**: the Stalybridge to Huddersfield Railway was built from 1846–49, and involved tunnelling through Standedge, running parallel to the earlier canal tunnel. Eventually three 3-mile (4.8-km) railway tunnels were built, opening in 1849, 1871 and 1894, and at one time around 2,000 men were employed in their construction.

Now follows a long, tiring climb out of the Tame Valley towards Standedge. The track ascends steadily through stone-walled fields to pass to the left of the solid, renovated farmhouse at Diggle Edge. Join the tarmac drive uphill; almost immediately bear right **D** off it through a bridlegate onto open rough grass-land. Keep uphill on a narrow grassy path, with a wall on the left. The path bears left to pass behind huge spoil heaps, eventually turning sharp left to pass a house with boarded-up windows on the right: it's an eerie and desolate place. Note the air shaft **46** for the tunnel on the left. The rough track curves left and continues towards the road; stay on the track where the Standedge Trail goes straight on. Pass to the left of a metal gate, and go ahead to a wooden gate to meet the A62 at Standedge cutting.

Cross carefully – even though huge signs on either side of the crossing should alert motorists to the approaching Pennine Bridleway, and visibility is good in decent weather, traffic tends to move very swiftly along these trans-Pennine roads. Go through another gate, then bear right, keeping the stock fence on the left, and follow this across open grassland to a T-junction of paths; turn left along a stock-fenced track, joining the route of the Pennine Way **47** for a brief moment. The track rises up then descends gently, becoming wide and rocky, to meet Standedge Foot Road on a bend. Keep straight on – this is a quiet lane that drops towards the A62. Pass two bridleways leading right; just after the second one turn right **E** between cottages along Bleak Hey Nook Lane.

The busy A roads are, thankfully, soon left far behind as this narrow tarmac lane wends its way downhill, passing Old School House on the right. Castleshaw Lower Reservoir comes into view left; the village that can be seen in the distance beyond the reservoir is Delph, in 1851 linked by a small branch line to the railway at Uppermill. This was charmingly known as the 'Delph Donkey', endorsing local tradition that the carriages were horse-drawn. Pass Castleshaw House on the right, and continue along Dirty Lane towards the reservoir. The site of Castleshaw Roman fort **48** can be found nearby on the left, dating from around AD 80 and marking the line of the military road from Chester to York.

Where Dirty Lane bears away left, keep right along Castleshaw Top Bank, running along the top of the dam between Castleshaw Upper and Lower Reservoirs (construction began in

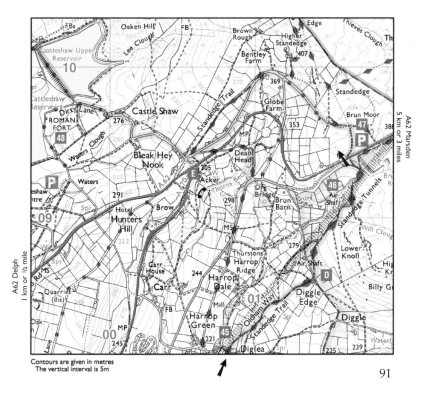

Contours are given in metres
The vertical interval is 5m

Looking back along the Pennine Bridleway over the Piethorne Valley. The trail from the A6

r The Ram's Head Inn can be seen top left.

1891). Turn left along a walled track to meet another track on a bend, with houses ahead left. Turn right through a gate and continue up a very steep, tiring, walled and stony track – Low Gate Lane – that climbs steadily uphill, eventually passing through a gate to reach a junction of tracks and paths. Turn right **F** through a five-bar gate, and on along a rough walled track (Moor Lane). Where the track ends, pass through a gate onto open moorland. Turn left **G** on the made-up path, following a broken-down wall on the left downhill to reach a holding area and gate on the A640 Huddersfield Road – an 18th-century turnpike road – opposite Dowry Reservoir. This is one of the Denshaw group of reservoirs, built between 1875 and 1883. Rumour has it that circus elephants from Manchester were used to help during construction! Cross with care, and continue downhill, turning right on meeting the track heading towards the bridge at the head of the reservoir.

Cross the bridge, and go through a gate; keep uphill and through another. Continue up the steep, walled track – Dowry Road – and through a wooden gate. Keep going uphill; where the walls end, turn right through a bridlegate to the right of a five-bar gate, and immediately through another; turn right and follow the wall on the right along the edge of grass moorland. This lovely, grassy track runs along the contours below Lurden Top, rising to 1,406 feet (429 metres) above left. The track levels off as Rape Hill **49** hoves into view ahead, to reach a T-junction of tracks.

Turn left **H** downhill and follow the track to reach Readycon Dean Reservoir; bear left along its southern edge, then turn right

The flowerheads of common cottongrass – which thrives on boggy moorland – resemble tufts of cotton wool.

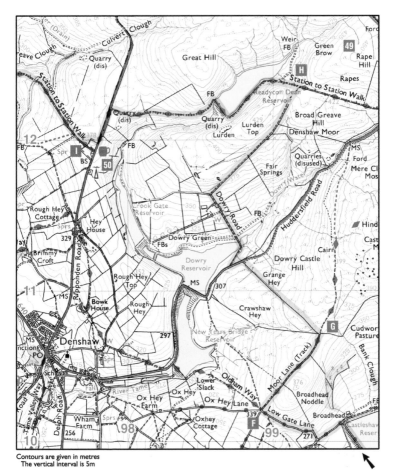

Contours are given in metres
The vertical interval is 5m

over the dam. The track bears left on the other side and runs gently downhill, above a deep clough below left. Pass through a bridlegate, with views to Crook Gate Reservoir left, and continue to meet the A672 Ripponden road (an old turnpike road); go through a wooden gate and turn left on a track running parallel to the road. Turn right to cross the road **50** – again, take great care. Go through a small gate and along an enclosed path. The path drops down a little and passes through a five-bar gate in a high wall. Turning left here will take you to The Ram's Head Inn.

Back on the trail, turn right **I**, with good views over Rooden and Piethorne Reservoirs – there are six reservoirs in all in the Piethorne Valley, with Piethorne itself the first to be constructed, in 1866. Continue along a broad gritty track. Where the track bears left to a farm keep straight on, passing stock pens on the left.

The intrusive Rakehead viaduct carries the busy M62 motorway high above Longden End Clough: something of a shock after the peaceful countryside traversed beforehand.

Pass through a bridlegate, and continue downhill; where a track bears away left, keep straight on downhill towards Piethorne Reservoir. The track rounds the head of the reservoir, joining the route of the Rochdale Way, a 50-mile (80-km) circular walking trail around the Borough of Rochdale; once on the other side, look right to see the dam of Norman Hill Reservoir. Pass through a metal gate on a gritty, high-walled track: the area of deciduous trees over the wall on the left is Old House Ground Nature Reserve **51**. This is another long, arduous climb; the track levels off a little between Turf Hill and Binns Pasture. Keep going – the traffic you can hear is on the M62, a mere ¹/₂ mile (0.8 km) away to the north. Then the path broadens and descends gently along Tunshill Lane, an old track. The track drops down; look right for an amazing view of the M62 Rakewood viaduct **52**, soaring 140 feet (43 metres) over the valley of the Longden End Brook.

At the next junction of tracks and paths – with Dick Hill (1,011 feet/308 metres) rising immediately ahead – turn right **J** through a bridlegate to the left of a five-bar gate, and continue along a broad, stony track, which curves right around the slopes of Nicholas Pike, then drops gently downhill. Pass through a bridlegate and over a stream, and then bear sharp left into the clough, with the brook on the right. The M62 is pretty intrusive all along this stretch – it's estimated that 90,000 people use this route across the Pennines every day, so it's incredibly busy and noisy. Pass a house and garden on the right, then a bridlegate, and keep going down the clough to pass derelict mill buildings on the right. The track broadens to an unmade lane as it sweeps right to pass under the viaduct. Be aware that the heavy traffic rumbles and clatters over the viaduct and may well startle horses – not to mention their riders!

Pass through a bridlegate to the left of a cattle grid, and continue downhill on what is now a private road – but public bridleway – passing the back of terraced houses on the left and an old mill building on the right, to reach Rakewood. The lane becomes tarmac and passes scattered mid-19th-century terraced cottages, with a leat below the lane on the left. This lane – Rakewood Road

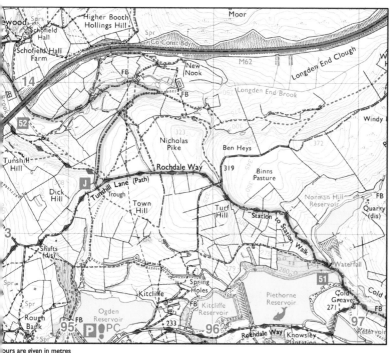

– runs along the edge of Hollingworth Lake **53** for about 200 yards/metres. Built in 1801 as one of six reservoirs supplying water for the Rochdale Canal, Hollingworth became known as the 'Weighvers' Seyport' in Victorian times. Then, as now, the lake was a focus for all kinds of entertainment, though pleasure gardens and paddle steamers have given way to watersports and nature trails.

Just past a small picnic area on the right (accessible for those on foot), turn sharp right **K** up Bear Hill. Stone setts give way to rough tarmac as the lane runs gently uphill; where a private lane 'footpath only' bears away right, keep straight on, passing a bungalow on the right. Continue along the private lane/public bridleway marked 'Syke & Sheep Bank Farms only', passing through a bridlegate by a cattle grid. The lane drops steeply downhill to reach renovated buildings at Syke Farm. Pass to the left of the buildings, then continue over a bridge and uphill on a broad, gritty track through an area of grass-covered hummocks – coal was once mined here – with a deciduous plantation on the slopes of Benny Hill to the right. Pass through gritstone gateposts: look out for the yellow 'driveguard' post in the middle of the track: not something any cyclist would wish to meet if coming downhill at speed. Continue uphill onto heather and grass moorland – another long haul. The track curves right around Benny Hill; where a path leaves it on the left, keep bearing right, eventually reaching a 'No Entry' sign on a gate on the right.

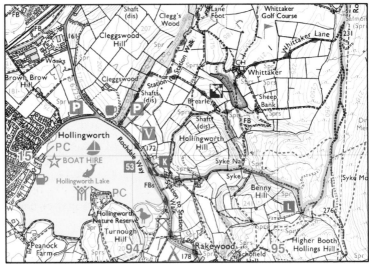

Contours are given in metres
The vertical interval is 5m

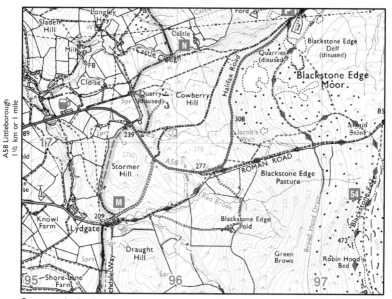

Contours are given in metres
The vertical interval is 5m

Turn left **L** here, bearing uphill; follow this narrow path to reach a junction of paths. Go straight over, following a line of pylons above right, across bracken-covered slopes. The path joins a track coming in from the right; bear left and keep going over Syke Moor. This is a lovely part of the route, gentle, open and airy, and with great views ahead towards the Rossendale Moors and the deep gorge at Summit, where the Mary Towneley Loop is joined. As the track drops a little, look up right to see the craggy outline of Blackstone Edge **54**, rising to 1,549 feet (472 metres) on the route of the Pennine Way.

This is a lovely, long, downhill run for cyclists. The track runs into a farm lane; bear right and keep along the lane. Look ahead to see the Pennine Bridleway rounding the left slopes of Stormer Hill. The track joins tarmac Whittaker Lane; keep ahead, downhill. Leave the moorland via a field gate by a cattle grid, and continue down a walled farm lane to meet the road at Lydgate, on the course of an old packhorse route – marked on OS maps as a Roman road, although this is unproven – over the Pennines. Turn right for 100 yards/metres; just after the bridge over Red Brook, turn left **M** on a broad track; where it bears right to a shed keep straight ahead, towards the pylon, to a fingerpost. Bear right along a rough raised path around the contours of Stormer Hill, parallel to a wall on the left. There are

Craggy gritstone outcrops on top of Leach Hill, with a glimpse of Chelburn Reservoir beyond. The Mary Towneley Loop is but a stone's throw away.

clear views towards Calderbrook, with its distinctive church spire, and the Summit gorge **55**, ahead. Follow the path as it drops steeply off the back of Stormer Hill to meet the holding area on the A58 Halifax Road.

Cross over and follow the raised, stony path through rough grassland. The path bears left and drops to meet a T-junction; turn right on a rough track through an area of scattered farms and rough walled fields. The track splits as it runs towards Castle Clough; keep left **N** on the lower fork and follow the track over the stream and then uphill to pass a faded blue bungalow on the left. The track continues towards a white farmhouse – the Field of Dreams retirement home for animals – with views over Higher Chelburn Reservoir to the left. Just before the archway into the yard, turn right through a new wooden gate, and left along a wide, grassy, fenced path that runs above the farm buildings, negotiating a number of peacocks en route; there are horses in the paddocks on either side of the path. Pass through double gates,and follow the fenced path – which is unsurfaced – as it bears left through more double gates, finally climbing steeply to a gate on the top of Leach Hill. Pass through the gate and follow the line of the route, which is waymarked across the open moor, crossing a timber sleeper bridge and eventually dropping fairly steeply downhill to meet a track just below the dam of Higher Chelburn. Turn right on the rough track to pass Lower Chelburn Reservoir (left), passing the dam and then going through a gate. Follow the main track downhill – ignore a track leading off right – to cross the reservoir outflow. Continue downhill across a rough turning area, to reach the Rochdale Canal **56** at Summit Lock, a delightful oasis, especially in summer when the lock-keeper's house is bedecked with window boxes and hanging baskets. The Summit pub can be found just over the canal on the left – another welcome sight! This is the highest point on the Rochdale Canal (originally opened in 1804, closed in 1952 and re-opened in 2002), at just over 600 feet (1,969 metres) above sea level.

Cross the bridge over the lock and continue uphill to reach the A6033 **O**. Cross at the Pegasus crossing; turn right along the broad pavement for about 20 yards/metres. By Windy Ridge (a house on the left) turn left up a very narrow path, rising steeply to reach a grassy area by a house. Keep straight on to pass between the house on the right and stables left, to meet the drive. Continue uphill to reach the Mary Towneley Loop **P**, and the end of the linear section of the first part of the Pennine Bridleway.

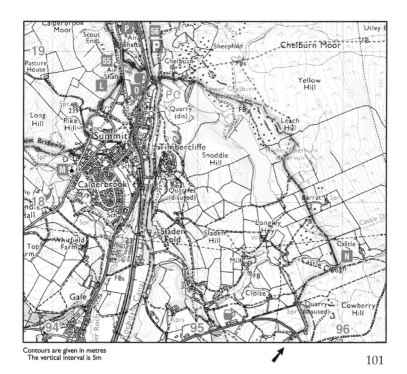

Contours are given in metres
The vertical interval is 5m

Modern-day long-distance Pennine routes

After a day on which a good number of both ancient and more recent trans-Pennine routes have been encountered, it seems appropriate to take a quick look at the other long-distance routes in the area. As well as the Pennine Bridleway, three other routes offer good opportunities for exploration. The information below, supplied by the Countryside Agency, gives a brief outline of each one.

THE PENNINE WAY NATIONAL TRAIL

268 miles (431 km)

Where is it?
The classic long-distance walk along the highest levels of the Pennine Hills. You need to be fit, well equipped and able to navigate. The Pennine Way runs from Edale in the Peak District National Park to Kirk Yetholm in the Scottish Borders, and takes around 14–16 days to walk.

What's it like?
Hilly, mainly untamed moorland cut with valleys, gorges and waterfalls. Few other people will be encountered away from market towns, villages and Hadrian's Wall. Strenuous, including climbs over Great Shunner Fell, Cross Fell and other peaks. Peat bog can be soaking in places. The route is waymarked, but use of a map is essential; compass work may well be needed.

Logistics
B&Bs, campsites, pubs, youth hostels and places to buy goods unevenly spread, so you need to plan certain sections. Maps, guidebooks, luggage transfer and packaged holidays available. Train and bus links to Edale, bus links only from Kirk Yetholm. Also train and bus links to Horton-in-Ribblesdale as an intermediate start point.

THE PENNINE CYCLEWAY

350 miles (560 km)

Where is it?
The longest of the National Cycle Network routes, along quiet lanes and traffic-free paths up the spine of northern England; you'll need a full range of gears. Runs from Derby to Berwick-upon-Tweed and takes around 8–10 days' cycling.

What's it like?
Runs through the beautiful countryside of the Peak District, Yorkshire Dales and Northumberland National Parks, North Pennines Area of Outstanding Natural Beauty and South Pennines. Unspoilt towns and villages, Hadrian's Wall and the River Tweed. Strenuous, largely on country lanes; some traffic-free paths and tracks; numerous steep climbs and descents. Route (68) well signed in both directions. Well-geared cycle in good working order essential.

Logistics
B&Bs, campsites, pubs, youth hostels and places to buy goods are unevenly spread, so you need to plan certain sections. Maps, guidebook and packaged holidays available. Train and bus links to Derby and from Berwick; intermediate starting points such as Hebden Bridge, Settle, Kendal (Oxenholme) and Appleby.

THE TRANS PENNINE TRAIL
215 miles (346 km)

Where is it?
The easiest of the four named Pennine routes, a coast-to-coast ride or walk through a rewarding mix of urban and rural heritage and culture. Runs from Southport on the Irish Sea coast to Hornsea on the North Sea coast; takes about 5–7 days to cycle, and 7–10 days to walk. Some sections suitable for horse-riding.

What's it like?
Runs along the famous River Mersey, through the Peak District National Park, past delightful villages, castles, abbeys and minsters, and the many attractions of Liverpool and Hull. Historic York an optional detour. Gradients mostly easy; well-surfaced traffic-free sections and minor roads. Well signed in both directions (routes 62 and 65 of the National Cycle Network). Semi-slick tyres recommended.

Logistics
Plenty of B&Bs, pubs, youth hostels, campsites and places to buy food. Maps and guidebook available. Train and bus links to Southport; bus and taxi only from Hornsea; train and bus links to Liverpool and Hull as intermediate start and finish points.

Further information and contacts, see the Useful Addresses section (page 168).

THE MARY TOWNELEY LOOP

The Pennine Bridleway is still under development and will eventually extend northwards from the Mary Towneley Loop. When the next section opens users may choose to follow the east or west side of the Loop to rejoin the linear route north.

The Mary Towneley Loop is a circular route and does not have a definite start or finish point. This guidebook directs users round the Loop in a clockwise direction, and is split into three sections, based around those places offering a good range of accommodation for people with horses. Walkers and cyclists can

The dark brooding gritstone crags of Cludders Slack can be seen above the Pennine Bridleway at Widdop.

be more flexible. Accommodation for all types of user is available all around the route, so individual itineraries can be constructed easily, depending on how far you want to go each day. The route description starts at Broadley, near Whitworth, but users coming from the southern linear section will arrive at the Loop at Summit. To reach Broadley from Summit, turn left onto Calderbrook Road and follow the directions given for the latter part of the Blackshaw Head to Broadley section (page 144). The Summit to Broadley section is 6 miles (10 km) long.

6 Broadley to Lumb

10 miles (16.1 km)

Make sure you pick good weather for this section. Much of the route crosses open moorland, following stone-setted Rooley Moor Road to Top of Leach, and on a damp, misty, bleak day it will feel like a long trudge through pretty uninspiring surroundings. Cyclists will be able to push on, but horse-riders and walkers cannot. Tackle this on a bright, sunny day, however, and you will enjoy some spectacular views and experience a fantastic feeling of space. A word of advice for walkers on the approach to Waterfoot: unless you are planning to stop for refreshments or supplies, you can easily work out a different and more rural route to avoid this urban section. The official Pennine Bridleway for horses and cyclists through Waterfoot crosses the A681 at a Pegasus crossing and then runs through the back streets, but walkers don't need to stick to this. It is clear from the OS map that several footpaths link with the Pennine Bridleway during its descent from Black Hill; the same can be said of the area to the north of Waterfoot, where the Pennine Bridleway runs up the eastern side of the Whitewell Valley.

The Pennine Bridleway reaches the edge of Broadley on Highgate Lane; turn left along Highgate Lane **A**, following signs to Healey Dell. Around 150 years ago the straggling hamlet of Healey Stones was a pretty rough place. Populated by colliers, handloom weavers and delphmen (quarrymen, from *delf*, the Old English word for 'quarry'), many of whom refused to work on Saturdays and Mondays, it was sarcastically nicknamed 'London', and was renowned for nude kicking competitions! This spectacle – frequently highly injurious, and sometimes fatal – took place on The Green, a field opposite the chapel, with the opponents naked apart from their clogs or boots. Contests were accompanied by wrestling matches, dog fights and racing, and the consumption of copious amounts of liquor. Indeed, it was said that 'the Sabbath was desecrated and made hideous by drunken orgies'.

Leaving all thoughts of such nefarious activity far behind, keep along the lane, which soon becomes tarmac and drops down through a residential area. At the T-junction turn right into Tonacliffe Road. At the next T-junction turn left **B** down Oakenshaw Avenue to reach the busy A671. Cross the road carefully, following signs for Catley Lane. Drop down the gritty path ahead, veering left, then right again, to run alongside the River

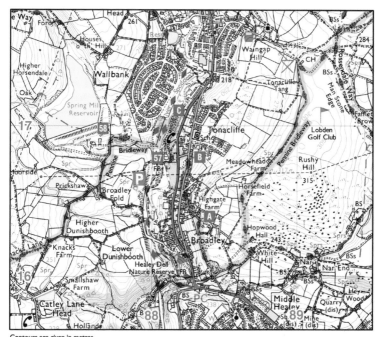

Contours are given in metres
The vertical interval is 5m

Spodden. The path continues through a nature reserve, with the river left. Established in 2003, there is a pond and viewing platform, and picnic tables. This peaceful spot is part of pretty Healey Dell Nature Reserve **57**, originally the site of several mills along the River Spodden, and holding the Rochdale–Bacup section of the now disused Lancashire and Yorkshire railway line, closed to all freight in 1967. Today it's a real oasis for wildlife; the intrusive main road is quickly forgotten. Look out for kingfishers and dippers along the river; you might see the great spotted woodpecker, great and longtailed tits, and willow warblers. Local schoolchildren and conservation groups were involved in helping to create the pond and wildflower meadows.

Turn left **C** to cross the river on a wide bridle bridge, then left again on a broad track, with the river on the left again. Where the track runs towards a metal gate ahead, turn right along another broad track, through an area of low-growing, scrubby vegetation. Follow the track through woodland, with a stream on the left, to pass through a line of posts. Meet a wide, gritty track coming in from the right. Keep left, and follow the track past the ruin of Spring Mill **58** (right), at the foot of the dam of Spring Mill Reservoir. Building work started here in

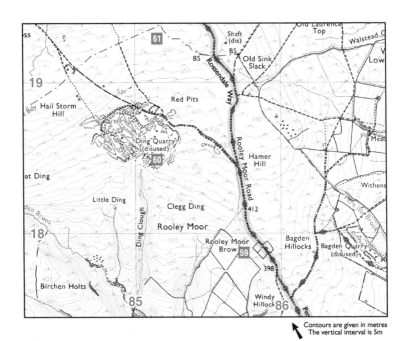

Contours are given in metres
The vertical interval is 5m

1871, part of a programme of reservoir construction on the Rossendale moors to improve water provision for the increased local population. It was much needed; in the 1850s the water supply in Rochdale had to be turned off for half the summer to conserve stocks. Note: this area is popular with flytippers, so look out for all manner of strangely shaped objects that may cause wary horses to shy. The track bears left away from the reservoir, and runs uphill on walled, cobbled Prickshaw Lane to the old farming hamlet of Broadley Fold. Turn right on cobbled Knacks Lane to pass through Prickshaw. Note the big arch in the centre of the building on the left. Originally built to allow access for wagons, these archways have now been incorporated into the fabric of many renovated cottages. This particular part of the Loop has a different feel compared with what is to come: many of the soot-blackened walls and dwellings typical of this part of the South Pennines have been cleaned up and 'gentrified'. Knacks Lane becomes tarmac and drops downhill to pass a white cottage, The Waste, on the right, before climbing up to the cattle grid and gate by Knacks Farm.

Keep straight ahead (along the middle one of three tracks) through a rough hillocky area, ignoring a track that joins sharp right, to meet a crossroads. Turn right **D** on Rooley Moor Road. This has to be one of the bleakest stretches of the Loop; it's amazing how quickly you feel as if you're in the middle of nowhere, despite the proximity of Rochdale. Rooley Moor Road – an ancient route from Burnley to Manchester – climbs steadily across lonely moorland for 2½ miles (4 km) to reach Top of Leach, at 1,555 feet (474 metres) the highest point within the Borough of Rossendale. Rooley Moor Road is largely made up of evenly laid setts, re-laid as part of a relief project for cotton workers during the 'Cotton Famine' of 1861–65. During the American Civil War supplies of cotton for local industry were severely disrupted, causing great hardship, particularly in the winter of 1862–63. On a good day, however, the views from the road are spectacular, stretching as far as the Clwydian Hills in North Wales, and north-east across the Whitworth Valley towards Stoodley Pike. Things weren't always so quiet here, however: Rooley Moor Brow **59** marks the site of The Moor Cock Inn, once known locally as 'The Rooleys', which fell into ruin in the 1930s. Disused Ding Quarry **60** (its spoil heaps may be spotted to the left of the track past Rooley Moor Brow) was once one of several quarries in the local-ity, and coal was also mined on the Rossendale side of the moor.

Follow the broad track – formed in places of two parallel lines of flags, worn down by the passage of wheeled vehicles – to pass to the right of Top of Leach **61**, with views over Bacup below right. If you're up here on a wet day it's worth remembering that

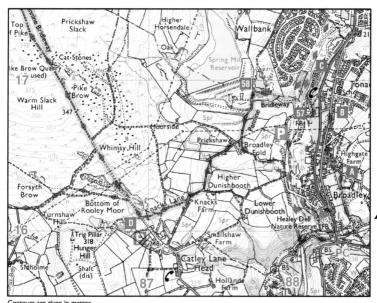

Contours are given in metres
The vertical interval is 5m

the Rossendale area has a higher rainfall than either the Dark Peak or the Yorkshire Dales! Note the engraved stone on the left of the path, commemorating the opening of the Rossendale Way – a walking trail – on 28 April 1985 **62**. The track drops slightly; where Rooley Moor Road goes straight ahead downhill, towards Stacksteads, bear left **E** and follow the track as it passes high above Cowpe Reservoir, constructed between 1901 and 1910. The chimney of Cowpe Mill **63**, a cotton mill dating from 1820, can be clearly seen below the dam. The track runs through derelict Cragg Quarry, a rather unattractive and eerie stretch of spoil heaps and old workings, with large pools of standing water. Haslingden Flag, a versatile building stone, was produced here. Where a gritstone wall comes in from the right, keep going downhill on the now gritty track, keeping the wall right. Pass through a five-bar gate and continue downhill on wide stone flags. At the next junction of paths bear right along the lower slopes of Black Hill, rising 1,391 feet (424 metres). The landscape opens up as Scout Moor is reached; local farmers have grazing rights here. At the next junction bear right again, slightly downhill.

Where the Rossendale Way bears away left on an embanked track (a dismantled tramway), keep ahead to pass through a five-bar gate **F** to leave the moor. Follow the now grassy track along the lower slopes of Black Hill, meeting a track on a bend; turn left downhill. Views over Rossendale **64** – the 'Golden

Cattle on Rooley Moor Road – possibly the only sign of life you'll see all day!

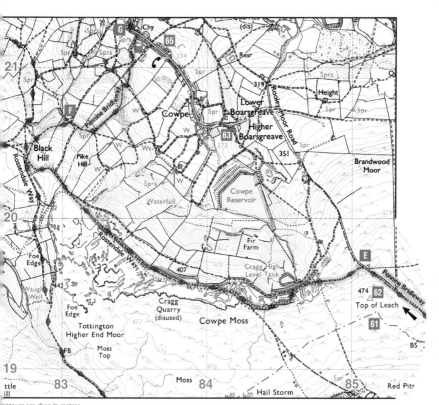

Contours are given in metres
The vertical interval is 5m

Valley' of the late 19th century – open up ahead; you get the feeling that you are returning to civilisation. Look out too for the distinctive outline of the Peel Monument, also known as Holcombe Tower, on Holcombe Moor, above Bury, erected in 1852 to celebrate the repeal of the Corn Laws. The Prime Minister at the time, Sir Robert Peel, was born at nearby Chamber Hall. As the track descends it becomes steeper and rockier, passing to the left of a deciduous plantation between stock fencing. It curves sharp right at Tippett Farm; continue downhill through a five-bar gate. Keep on down, with a fence on the left, to pass through a small wooden gate at the bottom of the hill. Follow the track down to meet the concrete drive leading to Tippett Farm. Bear right down the drive and keep on downhill to meet Cowpe Road, passing to the left of Brookland Terrace. (The Buck Inn **65** is a few yards to the right up Cowpe Road.)

Turn left **G** down Cowpe Road, passing the ruins of early 19th-century Lumb Holes Mill, which originally produced

Large sections of the Pennine Bridleway, particularly in the South Pennines area, follow safe, enclosed, walled green lanes, which are rarely – if ever – busy.

woollen cloth. Just past the cottages at Green Bridge South, turn right to cross the river on Lumb Holes Lane. Almost immediately bear left along terraced Bridge Street; at the T-junction turn left downhill on Carr Lane, site of a former textile mill. At the end of the lane rejoin Cowpe Road, turning right downhill to pass the restored Hugh Mill **66** (a fulling mill dating from the 17th century) on the right, and the Waterfoot Health Centre (formerly the site of the Bridge End feltworks) also on the right. Cross the River Irwell; just before meeting the busy Bacup Road, turn right along a cobbled and then gritty track, with the river and weir right and the coal yard left. Just before the end of the track turn left, keeping inside the fence, to reach the Pegasus crossing over the A681 **H**.

Cross over into the back streets of Waterfoot, typified by rows of back-to-back terraced houses. Continue up Townsend Street, which runs into Millar Barn Lane. Pass Bacup & Rawenstall Grammar School on the right. At the T-junction between Ye Olde Boot & Shoe on the left and The Jolly Sailor on the right, turn left down Booth Road. Just before the bridge over the Whitewell Brook, turn right along Todd Carr Road. At the end of the road – with the Kingdom Hall of Jehovah's Witnesses on the right – turn right uphill, and almost immediately right again under sycamores and limes on a made-up path which then bears left along the lower edge of Edgeside Park. The path drops to the road again after passing tennis courts on the right; keep ahead uphill on a track, bearing left in front of terraced cottages, with Woodside Close right. The track meets Edgeside Lane; turn left **I**. Pass Edgehill Baptist church and The White Horse public house on the right. Follow the road downhill, then up to the T-junction at Shaw Clough **J**.

Cross straight over, passing between two groups of terraced cottages on a tarmac lane which rises to pass through a metal gate at Shaw Clough Farm. Keep ahead, then bear right on a rough lane to pass Whitewell View bungalow on the left. The

Contours are given in metres
The vertical interval is 5m

113

track levels off; keep straight ahead, passing to the left of a restored building, with views over the Whitewell Valley opening up to the left. Much of this part of Rossendale was originally within the Forest of Rossendale, an ancient hunting ground governed by strict Forest Law: woe betide any commoner who attempted to poach game or steal fuel to help support his family.

Continue on between grassy banks, through a wooden gate, and then between walls. Follow the path along the top edge of a field, then through a small gate with Brock Clough Farm below left. The path drops slightly under twisted hawthorn trees, then rises up between grassy slopes, then stock fencing. It veers left a little and passes through a five-bar gate, with good views north up the valley, before becoming a low-walled track. Go through a five-bar gate and pass between a ruined building and cream-coloured house on the left, and stables right. Ignore a footpath to the left down the drive; keep straight ahead on a narrow grassy path. Pass through a wooden gate and continue to pass to the right of Thorn House Farm (another place where wary horses may need a bit of encouragement), and through another gate. The narrow path continues to run along the hillside, with a fence and field left dropping steeply down to the Burnley Road (constructed 1826) in the valley bottom. Pass

Looking from the Top of Leach over Cragg High Level Tank and Cowpe Reservoir to the mill hamlet of Cowpe, and the Rossendale Valley beyond.

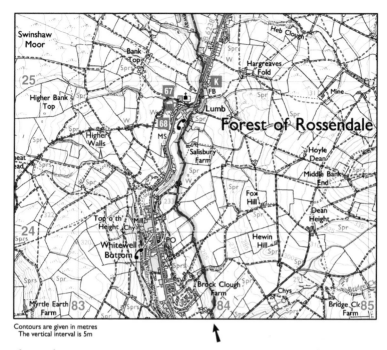

Contours are given in metres
The vertical interval is 5m

through a five-bar gate, and continue under trees with wooden palings on the left. Keep on to join a gritty track, ignoring a small path dropping steeply away left. Noting Lumb's parish church of St Michael **67**, built in 1848, on the other side of the valley, continue on the track, which becomes tarmac, to cross the Whitewell Brook on a bridge. Turn immediately right along a grassy track running between the brook and Lumb Valley Rest Home, which was a school from 1871–1952. (NB If in desperate need of refreshment, keep straight on here to the road and turn left for The Hargreaves Arms **68**, a few yards down the road.) The grassy track meets the B6238 at Lumb Bridge **K**.

Cross the road and turn right, and almost immediately left up tarmac Peers Clough Lane. The pretty 3-acre (1.2-hectare) Lumb Millennium Green is found here on the left, with a pond, walkways, picnic area and benches. Originally neglected land, it was opened in September 2000 and now provides ideal habitats for all manner of birds, butterflies, mammals and amphibians. You may see the extraordinary heron flying here from the Whitewell Brook, or – depending on the time of year – summer-visiting house martins, swallows and swifts. The old Lumb toll house, dating from the mid 19th century, used to stand on the corner of Peers Clough Lane.

Rossendale's 'Golden Valley'

Originally a small-scale wool-weaving area in the 17th century, successful conversion to mechanised cotton production by the late 18th century lead to Rossendale becoming known as the 'Golden Valley' in the latter half of the 19th century on account of its industrial wealth. 'Cotton Lords' – often hardworking and enterprising local men, who started out as millworkers – made the most of and profited from the new opportunities. These cotton 'pioneers', such as the Whitehead brothers of Rawtenstall – the largest town in Rossendale – were responsible for building many of the mills and civic buildings that can still be seen in the valley towns today. The woollen industry never quite disappeared, however, and in the late 19th century the wool-felt trade developed, first producing slippers, which became more valuable to the area than the textile industry, and then all kinds of footwear. Felt is still made today, and the footwear industry continues to produce boots and shoes.

The Pennine Bridleway runs through the back streets of Waterfoot, and the fortunes of this small town have been inextricably linked to the changing fortunes of its industrial status. Situated on the River Irwell at the western end of Thrutch Gorge – carved through the gritstone by powerful rivers, fed by glacial meltwaters at the end of the last Ice Age – Waterfoot developed as an early industrial village. The settlement's physical location, on a powerful natural water supply, rendered it suitable as a site for the mechanised production of wool and later cotton. Steam power came late to the area, owing to the lack of readily available coal and to the number of streams capable of powering small mills – by 1830 the rivers of Rossendale supported more than 45 of these. Until the coming of the Manchester–Rawtenstall Railway in the mid 19th century, enabling bulk supplies of coal to be brought into the area, coal had to be dug out of pits on the moors above and transported to the valleys along short tramways or 'coal lanes'. Coal mining in Rossendale has all but stopped now.

It is hard to imagine the prosperous times of the 'Golden Valley' today – the cotton industry went into serious decline at the start of the 20th century. Many of the derelict mills and factory buildings, however, have found a new lease of life as museums, or centres for small businesses, and Rossendale is working hard to reinvent itself as a tourist destination.

Apart from some road crossings, on the whole the bridleway round the Loop keeps well away from traffic. This section, close to a local railway, is short and well fenced.

117

7 Lumb to Blackshaw Head

18 miles (29 km)

Today's section of the Pennine Bridleway is wonderfully varied. The route moves swiftly away from the valley of the Whitewell Brook and later the relative security of the Cliviger Valley at Holme Chapel to round the top of the Loop across the remote moorland of north-west Calderdale, studded with dramatic, dark outcrops of gritstone. En route the Lancashire/Yorkshire boundary is crossed, and soon after that the Pennine Bridleway meets the Pennine Way briefly. All users will appreciate the fact that the route follows an old packhorse trail across this section, so aiding navigation in times of rain and mist. There is a real feeling of remoteness up here – one can almost imagine meeting a string of packhorses, loaded with cloth or coal. It should be mentioned that early on – from the top of Peers Clough Lane all the way to Holme Chapel – a large number of gates have to be negotiated. Fortunately most of these are long-handled bridle-gates that can be relatively easily dealt with from horseback, depending, of course, on the height of your mount, and the experience levels and patience quota of both horse and rider.

From the B6238 in the centre of Lumb **A,** the Pennine Bridleway proceeds up Peers Clough Lane (at one time known as 'Bob's Shop Lane'). The surface soon becomes gritty; keep going gently uphill. Pass farm buildings on the right, go through a field gate, and proceed uphill between high banks; the track levels off and becomes more open. Turn right through a small metal gate, and enjoy views ahead of the hills beyond Clough Bottom Reservoir **69** (constructed between 1891 and 1896). Pass through another bridlegate to follow a section between banks, and through another bridlegate; keep on along the edge of a field, with a low wall on the right. Note how the undulating rough farmland here is characterised by a network of broken-down gritstone walls; it gives the area a feeling of abandonment. At the end of the field go through the bridlegate to meet a junction of paths, with a track to Water leading right and Chamber Height Barn across the field to the left.

Go through the five-bar field gate ahead and turn sharp right **B** to take the grassy path along the edge of the field, with a bank and hawthorn hedge right. Go through the next bridlegate, soon descending downhill – stony underfoot – to go through a small wooden bridlegate and over a spring on a broad bridge. The path

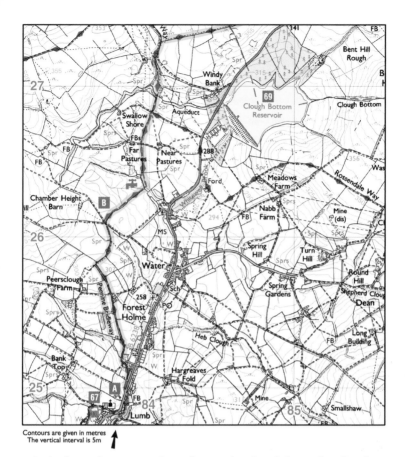

Contours are given in metres
The vertical interval is 5m

winds through an area of rough grassland and through a five-bar gate; note the boggy area below the path to the left. Follow the path gently uphill to meet the track linking the houses at Far and Near Pastures, and cross it via two gates.

The broad track runs uphill to cross another track and go through a metal gate, where it joins the 45-mile (72.5-km) Rossendale Way walking route for a short while. Continue uphill on a broad gritty track to another gate under a lone sycamore tree; Lower Cross Farm used to stand here. The track continues over an old aqueduct, part of the catchment area for the reservoir, and under a line of pylons. This is part of the old packhorse track from Rochdale to Clitheroe, which continued south to pass over Rooley Moor; finished cloth would be taken via this track south to Rochdale market for sale. Follow the track along the edge of a small clough (below left), with the odd twisted hawthorn tree on the right. Cross a gritty track and

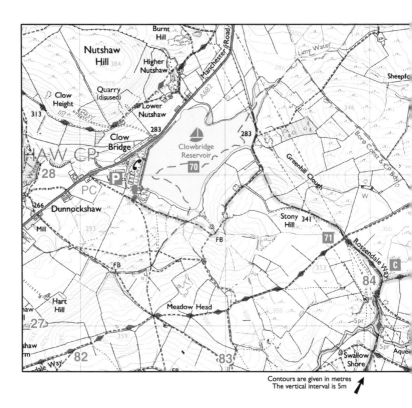

Contours are given in metres
The vertical interval is 5m

keep straight ahead to reach a junction of paths after 50 yards/metres. The Rossendale Way continues straight ahead. A bridleway from Clowbridge Reservoir **70** (completed 1865, and now with toilets, horsebox parking area, hitching rail and water supplies) joins the Pennine Bridleway at this point (a little way along this bridleway may be found Compston's Cross **71**, restored in 1902 at the meeting point of ancient trackways on Gambleside Moor). Clowbridge Reservoir is one of the recommended horsebox parks for the Loop.

The Pennine Bridleway turns right **C** through a wooden bridlegate and passes through a broken-down gritstone wall; continue on the track as it runs through rough grassland along the edge of Red Moss, on the slopes of White Hill, keeping the wall on the right. This is a lovely, open, airy track; note the deciduous plantation across the wall right, and picnic tables. This is Dunnockshaw Community Woodland **72**, part of the Forest of Burnley project (started in 1997), which will double the amount of woodland in the borough through a programme of new planting and restoration of existing woodland. It is estimated

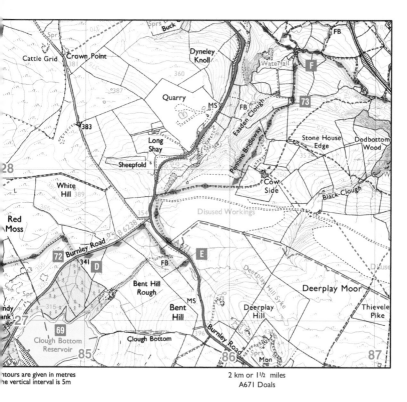

Contours are given in metres
The vertical interval is 5m

2 km or 1½ miles
A671 Doals

that by Roman times burning and grazing had reduced the natural forest cover of the area to only 20 per cent; that figure has since fallen to below 3 per cent. There are two waymarked circular bridleway trails accessible from the Pennine Bridleway here, as well as a number of walking routes.

Follow the line of the wall; where it ends, go through a bridlegate, then turn sharp right down a fenced track. Pass through a metal five-bar gate and cross the B6238 – it's relatively quiet. New woodland is also being created around Clough Bottom Reservoir on the other side of the road, through which an eco-trail has been established.

Turn left **D** through a five-bar gate and continue parallel to the road, with a wire fence left. About 50 yards/metres from the T-junction with the A671 Burnley–Bacup road, which is busy, follow the track right to run parallel with it. Note the views towards the great treeless expanse of Worsthorne Moor opening up to the north. The track crosses a stream on a broad bridge; where a broken wall runs across the track, turn left to meet the A671 through a wooden gate.

121

Cross the road carefully, pass through another gate, and turn left **E** parallel to the road, going through a five-bar gate en route. The track runs gently downhill, turning right to run along the east flank of steep-sided Easden Clough (where there is an area of millennium project planting). Good views open ahead over Southward Bottom in the Cliviger Valley. The track runs towards Cow Side Farm; 50 yards/metres before the farm is reached, bear left along a path. This undulating, grassy path rejoins the farm track; keep straight on, dropping downhill, passing through a five-bar gate. Where the track curves to the left, marked 'Private', turn right through a gate in to the field. The memorial to Mary Towneley, after whom this part of the Pennine Bridleway is named, is straight in front of you **73**. It's a good place to stop for a minute, and to enjoy the inspirational quote that has been carved on the memorial: 'The air of heaven is that which blows between a horse's ears'. Directly beyond the memorial can be seen the wind farm on the edge of The Long Causeway (an ancient highway) which will be passed later on this section. Look north-west and you will see the urban sprawl of Burnley; look east for views over Holme Chapel in the Cliviger Valley. The distinctive outline of Pendle Hill, rising to 1,826 feet (557 metres), can be seen beyond Burnley, infamously linked with witchcraft in the early 17th century; stories of the Pendle Witches intrigue visitors to this day.

From the memorial, turn left and go steeply downhill along the left edge of the field, then zig-zag down to a metal gate. Go through this, and with a white cottage, Stone House Fold, on your left, turn right **F** along a rough track to pass to the left of a ruined building between broken-down walls. Where the walls end, keep ahead on a rough track along the lower slopes of Stone House Edge, which rises quite steeply above the track on the right. The track runs through a gate to the left of Scout Farm (1868), and along the edge of a field to another gate. Go through this and turn left on a farm track. Where this bends sharp left towards an underpass for the Burnley–Todmorden railway line, keep straight on across grassland. The next wooden gate leads to a track that runs right alongside the railway, before rising slightly above it. Riders of nervous horses should keep a watch out for trains here – thankfully this is only a short section and can be negotiated quickly.

Turn sharp left **G** to pass under the railway, and immediately right on a track to pass beneath sycamore and horse chestnut. This meets a lane; turn left along a walled lane to cross the River Calder – unusual in that it splits fairly near its source, and then flows both east and west – and follow the lane to meet the A646

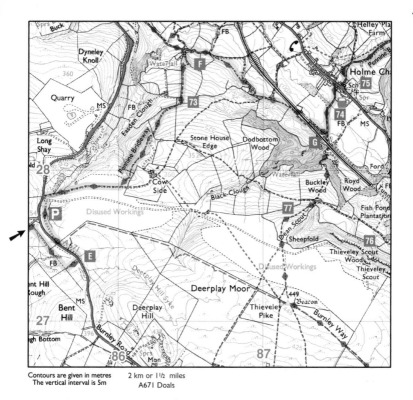

Contours are given in metres   2 km or 1½ miles
The vertical interval is 5m   A671 Doals

at Holme Chapel. The lane passes the way into The Ram Inn **74** (built in 1691, and formerly a farm) en route, with a good beer garden and facilities for horses too. This part of the Cliviger Valley (named after the ancient parish of Cliviger) is also undergoing a transformation as a result of the Forest of Burnley project. Over 74 acres (30 hectares) have been planted with native species – sessile oak, rowan, birch, alder, cherry and ash – and parts of the valley sides have been fenced as protection from over-grazing and to allow regeneration of heather and bilberry.

The church of St John the Divine **75**, consecrated in 1794, may be found just beyond the pub on the other side of the road. It replaced a 16th-century chantry chapel, which was demolished by Thomas Dunham Whitaker, squire of Holme, in 1788, and whose family largely funded the construction of the new church. In the late 18th century a later Dr Whitaker had half a million trees planted on his estate, resulting in much of the mature woodland that can be seen here today (though he was also responsible for non-native species such as sycamore and rhododendron). He would no doubt have been delighted at the

The strange, almost lunar landscape of Sheddon Clough, where evidence of limestone excavation remains in the form of grass-covered hillocks or 'hushings'.

Forest of Burnley project! The churchyard at Holme has some interesting inhabitants, including General Sir James Scarlett, commander of the Heavy Brigade at the Battle of Balaclava in 1854, and Henry Wood, native of Cliviger and a clerk of works during the rebuilding of St Paul's Cathedral. He was buried at the chapel on 1 November 1729, and in his will bequeathed the sum of one guinea to be paid annually on the preaching of a sermon – the 'Wood Sermon' – four weeks before Christmas.

Cross the road and turn right for a few yards, then turn left up the rough tarmac lane by the school. Where the lane bears left to Helly Platt Farm, turn right through a five-bar gate along walled Holme Chapel Road, an ancient highway. Look back to the right for fantastic views over part of the Cliviger Gorge, and sandstone Thieveley Scout Crags **76** in particular. This impressive physical feature was formed millions of years ago, when movements in the earth's crust created a fault line in the Carboniferous shales and sandstones, creating a gorge running from Todmorden to Burnley. Meltwaters at the end of the last ice age widened and deepened the gorge, causing some parts to become unstable; subsequent landslips revealed seams of coal, giving rise to an important local mining industry. A couple of attempts at lead mining at Dean Scout **77**, on the other side of the valley, in the 17th and 18th centuries were unsuccessful.

Where the green lane drops down a little turn right **H** through a wooden gate. Follow the grassy track (soon joining a gritty track that comes in from the right) towards Merrill Head Farm; about 100 yards/metres before the farm turn right across open grassland, then left through a gate to walk along the left edge of Green Clough. Go through a gate at the top of the hill (Pearson's House Farm left) and cross rough grassland, with a fence on the right. Bear right through another gate, and right again, parallel to the road that follows the line of The Long Causeway towards the wind farm **78**. Turn left **I** through a gate to cross the road; turn right along the opposite verge for around 50 yards/metres, then left through another gate (with a horse stile) to enter open moorland, part of the European designated South Pennines Special Protection Area.

The next stretch is a sort of brief early warning, if you like, of things to come: as you strike off across this open moorland – haunt of ground-nesting birds such as lapwing, curlew and red-shank in spring – civilisation is suddenly left far behind. It would be a tough place in inclement weather. But surprisingly soon –

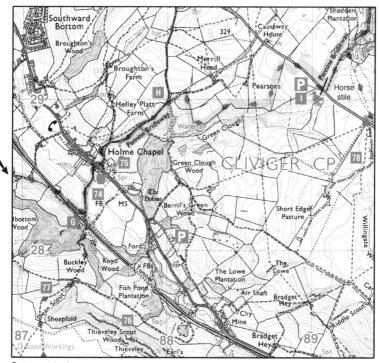

Contours are given in metres
The vertical interval is 5m

and just as you're beginning to feel that you really are the last person left on the planet – the track drops gently downhill towards pretty green oaks, conifers and beech trees in tranquil Sheddon Clough. Meet a wall on the left; join a gritty path and keep straight on to cross a stream on a bridge, then along an earthy walled track; note the strange grass-covered, tree-studded hillocks to the right. Sheddon Clough was an important source of limestone from medieval times, and this area of 'hushings' **79** results from open-cast mining activity. Limestone was burned with coal to produce quicklime, used to improve the naturally acidic Pennine soils for agriculture. It was flushed out by streamwater, dammed and then released – hence 'hushing'. The construction of the Skipton–Burnley section of the Leeds–Liverpool Canal in 1796, and hence cheaper supplies of limestone from further afield, heralded the end of the local industry.

Follow the walled track as it leaves the plantation behind; note clumps of rhododendrons appearing on the slopes on the left, planted by a 19th-century landowner as cover for game. Cross a stream on a wooden footbridge (or go through the ford); turn left, keeping the wall left, with a steep grassy hill right. Pass under two sycamores and over another stream to reach Shedden Heys; turn right **J** over the old packhorse bridge. Follow the track, with a stock fence left, to reach a gate and horse stile leading left over the dam of Cant Clough Reservoir. On the other side of the dam turn right through a bridlegate and horse stile, then left up a concrete road, which soon reduces to a track. The track drops down and curves right to reach Hurstwood Reservoir. Note that this area is likely to be busy; there is a car park and picnic area nearby, and the area is popular with cyclists and dog walkers.

Turn right **K**, and follow the broad, gritty track to the end of the reservoir. Where the Burnley Way (footpath) goes off left, keep straight on steadily uphill for a long stretch, crossing a stream on a wide stone bridge. At the junction of paths – with an area of new woodland left – turn right **L** to Gorple Road, an old packhorse trail. This broad, stony track – pretty rough in places – climbs steadily uphill before dropping down to cross the stream in Smallshaw Clough, then climbs again. This far north-west tip of Calderdale is mainly used as grouse moor and for sheep grazing; there are large expanses of blanket bog, with deep peat beds hugging the contours of the land, over layers of millstone grit and sandstone. This is a managed landscape: controlled burning of heather and grazing of sheep maintain the moorland cover. Keep an eye out for the day-flying short-eared owl quartering

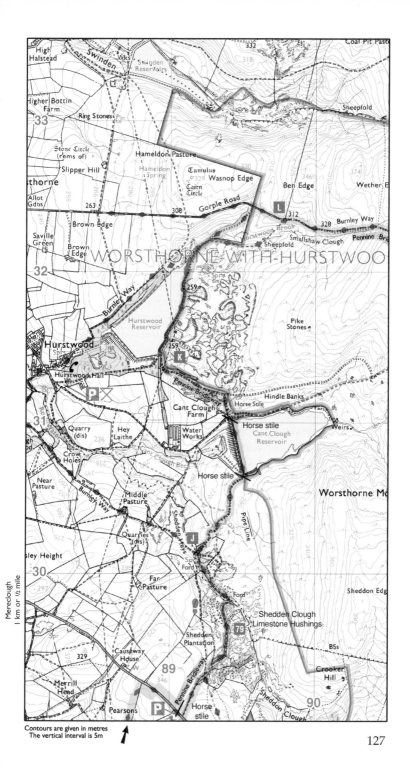

Merceclough
1 km or ½ mile

Contours are given in metres
The vertical interval is 5m

127

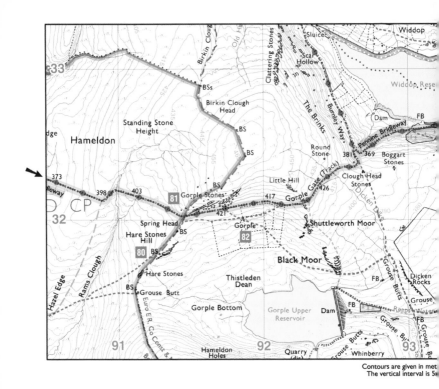

Contours are given in met
The vertical interval is 5m

the moor. This species nests in the area, and is entirely dependent on the short-eared vole; numbers of owls therefore fluctuate depending on the breeding success of the vole in any particular year. Other birds of prey here include the merlin – the smallest British bird of prey – which nest in reasonable numbers in the South Pennines. They have pointed wings and fly very fast after prey such as meadow pipits. Look out too for kestrels, with their characteristic hovering action, and also peregrine falcons (two to three times larger than the merlin). Look right to see the rocky outcrop of Hare Stones **80**, with expansive views across open moorland beyond, carpeted with purple heather in late summer.

The track curves left around the head of Rams Clough, then climbs uphill to Spring Head at around 1,380 feet (420 metres), where Lancashire is left behind and Yorkshire entered **81**, with views ahead towards craggy Gorple Stones and numerous gritstone outcrops. Broken-down walls and ruined buildings below the track on the right mark the site of Gorple Farm **82** on the slopes above Gorple Upper Reservoir (1927–34). The track continues on, and drops quite steeply towards Widdop ('wide valley') Reservoir, built between 1871 and 1878 to augment water supplies

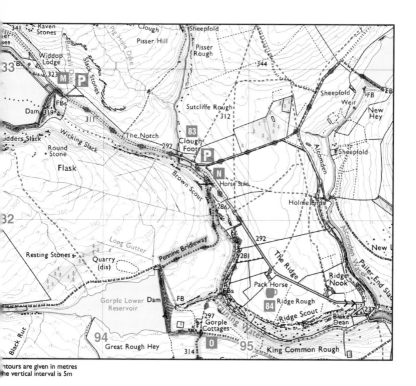

Contours are given in metres
The vertical interval is 5m

for Halifax. A temporary settlement – known locally as 'Navvyopolis' – was put up in this remote spot to house the navvies and their families. The track zig-zags downhill (between bilberry-covered slopes in summer), then turns sharp right to run along the southern side of the reservoir. Continue past a small coniferous plantation, then beneath the great blocks of The Cludders ('mass of rock') above the track on the right, before turning left over the dam on a broad paved causeway.

Pass through gates on the other side, and turn right **M** down a quiet tarmac lane (Halifax Road). Go downhill to the parking area on the left at Clough Foot **83**; here the Pennine Bridleway just touches the Pennine Way. The white building on the hill ahead is The Packhorse Inn **84**, on the old Burnley–Colne packhorse route.

Opposite the car park turn right **N** through a gate and horse stile, and follow the water board access road to Gorple Lower Reservoir (1927–34), with deeply incised Graining Water on the left. On reaching the dam, turn left across it; note the sign asking horses and cyclists to give way to estate traffic. Follow the road as it turns left to pass Gorple Cottages (a Water Board house), and turn right **O** (joining the Pennine Way) through a metal gate. Follow the steep, rough track uphill; at the next five-bar gate and horse stile the Pennine Way is signed left to Heptonstall Moor. Keep straight on to the top of the hill, from where the track starts to drop down at the head of the Colden Valley. Views suddenly open up down the valley – characterised by small walled fields and scattered dwellings – towards the tower of Heptonstall church, and to the distinctive outline of Stoodley Pike monument; the Pennine Bridleway passes just beneath this as it runs above the Calder Valley. Proceed downhill, with a high gritstone wall right, to pass through a field gate onto Edge Lane.

Follow Edge Lane gently downhill until a house called Longtail is reached on the left; the patchwork of green fields provides a pleasant contrast to the bleak moorland encountered earlier. Turn sharp right **P** downhill on School Land Lane – this is steep, and could be slippery for horses – where there is a sign to Land Farm Garden & Gallery **85**. (Those needing refreshment or provisions would do well to continue on along Edge Lane to visit May's Farm Shop: see page 132.) School Land Lane drops down to cross the Colden Water on Landbridge. Keep straight ahead on a rough track that runs to the right of and then left above the gardens. The path narrows and veers right uphill through a gate, then continues steeply uphill between banks to a bridlegate, and on along a grassy path to a field gate.

Go through the gate and straight over the farm drive, keeping Field Head Farm on your left, and through another gate, soon passing ponds and beehives below left. Continue along a grassy track, through a gate, and bear left downhill; the path bears right and rises steeply uphill to go through another gate. Follow the path round over a stone culvert beside a pond. Pass through the gate and proceed uphill, through another gate and along the edge of the grounds of the renovated buildings at Strines Clough above right. When the stables (with clock-tower) are in front of you, turn left **Q** to reach Brown Hill Lane.

Follow this as it descends gently to meet a tarmac road on a sharp bend. Go straight ahead downhill; as the road curves left just before The New Delight Inn at Jack Bridge **86**, turn right along a lane opposite the parking area (with a good expanse of grass on the left). The Colden Water runs below the lane on the left. On seeing some houses on your right, turn right **R** onto the short, steep tarmac path (with Shaw Bottom house on the left); where this track turns left, keep straight on up a long, straight, narrow path – this is the steepest climb of the day. Cyclists

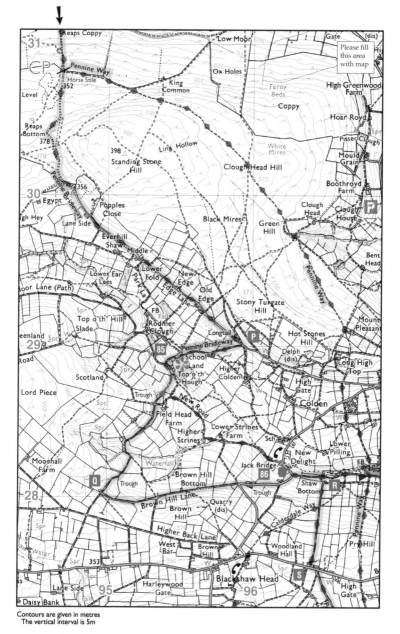

Contours are given in metres
The vertical interval is 5m

should note that a stone pillar has been placed almost in the middle of the path to mark the crossing point of the Calderdale Way (footpath) – not a good thing to meet if you were coming full tilt *down* this path! Follow the path up; it levels out and meets Badger Lane, Blackshaw Head **S**, between houses.

Changing times in the Colden Valley

This valley has a fascinating industrial history. It has long been used as a thoroughfare: Edge Lane, running up the east side of the valley, was an ancient track linking The Long Causeway to Reaps Cross, where it divided; one branch joined the road to Colne, and the other went up the Gorple Valley. The remains of Reaps Cross are situated just to the right of the Pennine Bridleway at the head of the valley.

The Colden Valley, in common with many others in the South Pennines, was once bustling with activity. From late medieval times to the early 1800s there was a flourishing hand-textile industry in these remote moorland valleys; families survived through a combination of self-sufficient farming and home spinning and weaving. The hand-textile industry declined dramatically between 1780 and 1840, when water-powered mills were built along the fast-flowing rivers. At one time there were 13 mills involved in spinning and weaving woollen and cotton cloth along a 5-mile (8-km) stretch of the Colden Water, which joins the River Calder at Mytholm, south of Heptonstall. By the 1850s most had augmented water power with steam power; coal for the Colden Valley mills came from open-cast mines on Stiperden Moor.

The last mill to be built (which was steam-powered) was at Jack Bridge; the chimney of Land Mill, a cotton mill built in 1805, can still be seen by Land Bridge. The highest textile mill in the valley, Rodmer Clough Mill, produced cotton goods; it was built around 1800 and demolished about 1890. The deserted farms in the upper reaches of the valley – an area known as Noah Dale – are a stark reminder of the effects of the Industrial Revolution: little by little the local population moved off the moors to settle and work in the industrial valleys below. There are some good examples of typical terraced weavers' cottages round about: stern, soot-blackened terraces with neat rows of large rectangular windows, constructed with the intention of giving as much light as possible to the handloom weavers of cotton, gingham and worsted. The odd hanging basket does little to soften these severe façades.

One of the more recent innovations in this tranquil valley is the lovely Land Farm Garden, which provides a welcome splash of colour in an area not renowned for its floral displays. It is open from May to the end of August, weekends 10am–5pm, and there is an entrance charge. You also must visit May's Farm Shop (or, as

Signs of the industrial heritage of the Calder Valley become increasingly apparent as the bridleway drops down into dark, dank Dean Delph, near Hebden Bridge.

it is appropriately known, 'Aladdin's Cave') at High Gate Farm on Edge Lane – just keep straight on (rather than turning down School Land Lane) and you'll soon find it. This extraordinary place was started in 1977 to supply the needs of local walkers and campers; today it is packed from floor to ceiling with everything you've ever wanted (as well as some things you'd never even thought about!), and May's bread-and-butter pudding has to be tasted to be believed. The shop is open from around 8am to 8.30pm every day, and has won various national awards.

8 Blackshaw Head to Broadley

18 miles (29 km)

Much of the Pennine Bridleway in the South Pennines follows a variety of old stone-setted packhorse trails and causeways, some thought to follow routes dating from pre-Roman times. They cannot be and should not be hurried along; they deserve to be treated with respect. For centuries – long before the coming of the turnpike roads in the 17th century, and later the canals and railways – they provided the main transport and communication links. On this section of the route the great contrast between the slow, peaceful pace of the old trails high up on the moorland edge, and the hustle and bustle of the industrial Calder Valley below, and later on the urban spread of Rochdale, becomes apparent. The cottages and gritstone walls passed en route are blackened with soot from the outpourings of the 'dark satanic mills', reminding one that the South Pennines lay at the very heart of the Industrial Revolution. The Pennine Bridleway also traces the routes of the Rochdale Canal and the main Manchester–Leeds railway line. It's a welcome relief to follow historic trails that keep well above these 19th-century (and later) developments.

From the end of yesterday's route, turn left along Badger Lane. After 50 yards/metres turn right **A** on a downhill track (look out for wild raspberries here in late summer), with fabulous views over the Calder Valley towards Stoodley Pike monument. Standing an impressive 120 feet (37 metres) high, and visible for many miles around – and an excellent landmark for checking progress around the Mary Towneley Loop – it was erected in 1856. An earlier version, erected in 1815 to commemorate the surrender of Paris after the Napoleonic Wars, was damaged by lightning and subsequently collapsed.

At the gate to Dove Scout Farm bear left downhill on a narrow packhorse trail between blackened gritstone walls. This zig-zags steeply down to meet a rough lane; turn right downhill through mixed deciduous woodland. The lane bears left and continues downhill, with a stream right. Note the terraces and stone facings visible amongst the trees here, evidence of the buildings, dams and sluices of the old Jumble Clough water-powered mill. The lane becomes gritty and passes between houses, then under the railway bridge to meet the A646 Hebden Bridge–Todmorden road. Turn left **B** just before

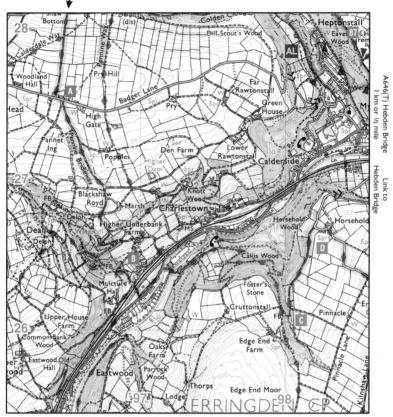

Contours are given in metres
The vertical interval is 5m

the road and continue along a fenced section, with a wall on the right. The road is busy, with a lot of heavy traffic – those with nervy mounts take care. After about 200 yards/metres turn right to cross the road at Callis Bridge where a Pegasus crossing is to be installed in 2004. Immediately cross the River Calder, and then the Rochdale Canal. The canal path can be used by walkers and cyclists to get to Hebden Bridge, where there are plenty of services and accommodation.

Continue uphill on a rough lane, which zig-zags up through Callis Wood, crossing a cattle grid/gate en route. Where Edge End Farm appears ahead, with a footpath to Stoodley Pike right, turn left **C** down a narrow path into woodland. The path crosses a stream on a packhorse bridge, goes through a five-bar gate, and rises along the top edge of Callis and Horsehold Woods under beeches and sycamore. On emerging into the open there are great views straight ahead of Heptonstall **87**. If you can ever

A lovely summer view of the compact and historic little village of Heptonstall.

manage it, this delightful hilltop village is well worth a visit – it's like taking a step back in time. Originating in the medieval period, Heptonstall developed as a handloom weaving village, and – protected from major industrial development on account of its physical location – is wonderfully preserved today. Only essential traffic is permitted to pass along its cobbled ways, lined with dark terraces of weavers' cottages; the last hand-loom weaver here died in 1902. Heptonstall has the oldest octagonal Methodist chapel still in use in the country, a ruined 13th-century church and a mid-19th-century replacement. One of the graveyard's more famous inhabitants is the poet Sylvia Plath. She was at one time married to the Poet Laureate Ted Hughes, who lived for a while at Lumb Bank, just north of the village on the edge of Colden Clough.

The path reaches a stone-setted lane (which leads downhill to Hebden Bridge); turn right to pass through Horsehold, an old handloom weaving hamlet and stopping place for packhorses (as evidenced by its name). Turn right **D** by Horsehold Farm. The cobbled way turns right and becomes tarmac, climbing gently uphill. Note the unusual tree-filled stone enclosures in the fields on the right. Turn right **E** along Kilnshaw Lane to pass Erringden Grange on the right; continue along the lane to pass Rough Head Farm, also right. The lane becomes gritty and walled; at a junction of tracks (with Kershaw and Lower Rough Head Farms right) keep straight on through a metal gate. The track ends at Swillington Farm; keep straight on, passing to the left of the farm, through a five-bar field gate and onto open moorland.

The Pennine Way crosses the Pennine Bridleway at this point. It's wonderfully open up here; the bustling Calder Valley is soon left far behind. Birdlovers will be interested to know that this area of the South Pennines moorland edge is the heartland of the British twite population; this exclusively seed-eating species feeds in traditional hay meadows. Surprisingly the European population is found only in England – mainly in the Pennines – and in Norway. The birds spend May to August on the moorland, and winter on the East Anglian saltmarshes.

Keep straight on along the old packhorse trail, London Road, which runs along the contours of the hill to pass below Stoodley Pike **88**; views over Todmorden open up in the valley

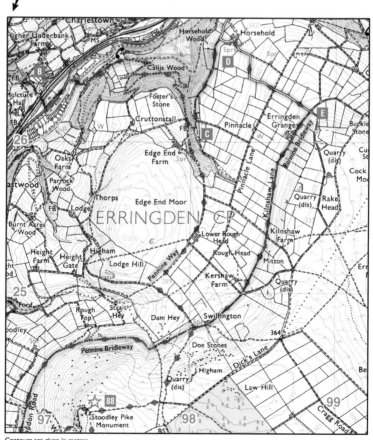

Contours are given in metres
The vertical interval is 5m

This view towards Calderdale was taken from the route of the Pennine Way by Stoodley P

route of the Pennine Bridleway lies out of sight on the lower slopes of the hill.

below right. Follow the trail as it drops down, eventually between stone walls, to meet a tarmac lane at right angles on the edge of the hamlet of Mankinholes. Turn right **F** – note the old water troughs on the right, with a circular section at either end, used for cooling milk churns as late as the 1970s. At this point the Pennine Bridleway joins the route of the Calderdale Way, a 50-mile (80-km) circular walking route, using many of the old packhorse trails, for a short stretch. Mankinholes was at one time a handloom-weaving settlement, linked by packhorse trails to markets at Halifax and Rochdale. It has a number of fine stone houses reflecting its comparative wealth: these were yeoman clothiers' houses, dating from the 17th century, one of which is now the youth hostel. A yeoman clothier was the

The old water tower at Lumbutts, with Stoodley Pike atmospherically silhouetted on the skyline.

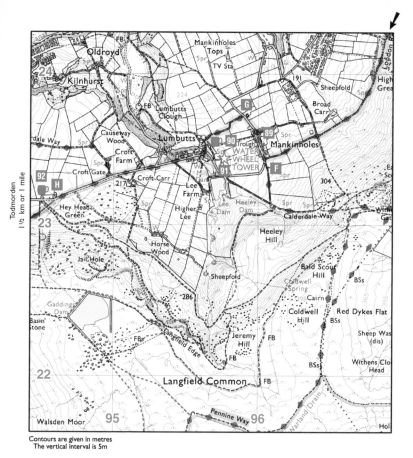

Contours are given in metres
The vertical interval is 5m

middle-man who supplied raw materials to local handloom weavers and collected the finished items for sale.

Pass the youth hostel **89** on the right; opposite the cemetery (right) turn left **G** along a narrow 'causey' ('causeway'), an old stone path leading to the water-powered mill at Lumbutts; today it passes The Top Brink Inn en route **90**. Pass the pub and car park on the left and continue along the causey, which drops steeply downhill to meet a tarmac lane (take care here). Turn right and follow the lane over the stream to pass Lumbutts Centre with its impressive 104-foot- (32-metre)-high water tower, formerly the site of a cotton-spinning mill **91**. The lane climbs steeply uphill. Where Hey Head Farm appears on the right, turn left **H** through a five-bar gate. (Note: if you are in need of refreshment and The Top Brink Inn was shut, keep straight ahead here to find The Shepherd's Rest **92** on the right; there are great views over Todmorden and beyond from its garden.)

The bridleway now follows the elevated causeway of Salter Rake Gate, a stone causeway packhorse route (originating in Saxon times) that runs along the contours and around Rake End. Many of the place names hereabouts give clues to the origins of hamlets or sites. A rake, for instance, is defined as a track that runs at an angle across a hill. Names such as Saltergate (gate comes from the Norse *gata*, for road or journey) give information about the packhorse loads: salt, for example, was brought inland from the coast and used for preserving food. The animals used most often on the Pennine packhorse trails were sturdy Galloways, a Scottish breed of pony (now extinct).

Once Rake End is past, good views open up over Walsden in the valley below. Here the three modes of transport along the narrow valley floor – road, rail and canal – can be clearly seen, crammed together. The track eventually passes through a metal gate by a house on the left, and continues to meet a tarmac lane on a bend at North Hollingworth Farm. Turn left along the lane, eventually passing to the right of a white house. Go through a field gate on a farm track onto open land; almost immediately bear right off the track on stone flags. Pass through a wooden gate, and follow the wall on the right steeply downhill – horses should take this gently – on a narrow causey. The path runs to the left of Dean Royd Farm, then along a level, grassy embanked stretch. Continue over a stream on a railed bridge, then climb uphill along another causey path and through a gate to reach the hamlet of Bottomley; there was a Quaker meeting house here in the late 17th century.

Turn right, and almost immediately bear right **I** (where the tarmac way enters Sweetbriar Cottage on the left) through a five-bar gate and down a very narrow, steep, walled, stone-setted path between fields. Take care: this can be slippery. The path runs between modern houses to meet a tarmac lane; keep straight ahead to cross the canal at Bottomley Lock. Follow the lane left over a stream, then right uphill to meet the busy A6033.

Turn left **J** along the verge to reach the Pegasus crossing (due to be installed in 2004), and cross over. Follow the fenced path, bearing right and uphill, to meet another track. Turn left, and continue along the grassy path. The huge sunken 'chimney' ahead is an air shaft marking the line of Summit Tunnel **93**, opened in 1841 for the Manchester–Leeds railway line. It's an amazing structure: you may well hear the muffled 'whoosh' of a train as it thunders under Calderbrook Moor. The tunnel is over 1¹/₂ miles (2.4 km) long, and was the first of its kind in the

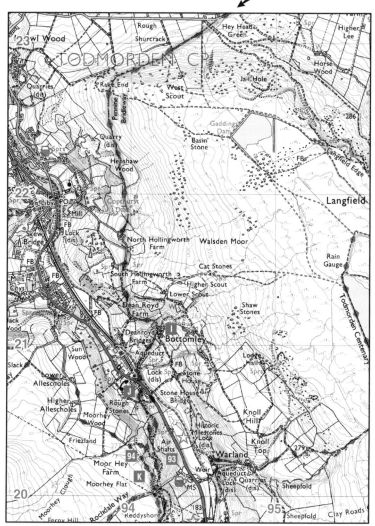

Contours are given in metres
The vertical interval is 5m

Pennines. Built by George Stephenson, it improved transport links between the industrial centres of Rochdale and the Calder Valley and beyond. The path leads through a gate, then zigzags very steeply uphill – those on horseback should be thankful! A milestone marks the top of the path, signing old routes to Todmorden, Rochdale, Burnley and Halifax **94**.

Turn left **K** along a broad, level track (a relief after the climb), passing under a line of pylons and through a metal gate. Continue, with a wall on the left and stock fence right.

143

Cyclists, near Calderbrook, riding the Loop anticlockwise. The southern part of the Loop is easily accessed and popular with cyclists and horse-riders just out for the day.

Pass through another gate; there are good views now towards Lower Chelburn Reservoir ahead; the Pennine Bridleway en route from Derbyshire runs along its edge. Take care over the next section: there is a very big drop off the path left over crags, but the path is broad **95**. Horses would be well advised to go in single file, and cyclists should go gently. The path joins a gritty track and drops gently downhill to join tarmac Calderbrook Road. Note the junction on the left where the Pennine Bridleway from Chelburn joins the Mary Towneley Loop **96**.

This is the point from which those joining the Loop from the south (see page 105) – and heading clockwise – should follow directions to Broadley.

Keep straight on along Calderbrook Road; after 50 yards / metres bear right **L** on a tarmac lane. Just before a metal gate and Water Board road ahead, bear left on a narrow fenced path between fields. This leads to a tarmac lane between houses and then fields on the edge of Summit, just a single dwelling until

144

the coming of the Rochdale Canal aided its development. Follow the lane as it bears left downhill, and turn right **M** by the iron gates of Calderbrook House.

From here all the way to Watergrove Reservoir cyclists will be able really to push on: the surface is good and the track undulates through rounded grass-covered hills. Follow the gritty track uphill; as it levels off look left for good views over the tall spire of St James's Church, Calderbrook, and then the ponds of the Pennine Trout Farm & Fishery. Follow the track to where it bears left into the yard at Grimes; keep straight on, passing to the right of the buildings, and through a field gate onto open grass moorland.

Follow the track as it bears away from the wall on the left. Pass through a field gate before dropping down to cross the stream in Turn Slack Clough – where horses can get a drink –

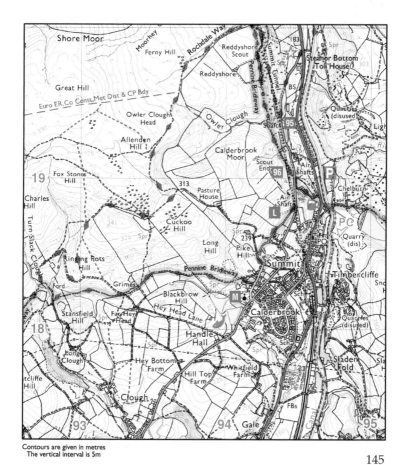

Contours are given in metres
The vertical interval is 5m

and proceed uphill again. The track continues along the contours before passing through a five-bar bridlegate in a wall. Turn left through the gate and follow the wall towards conical Ratcliffe Hill, bearing right with the wall to pass along its lower slopes. The track then curves round the end of High Lee Slack, passing a bridlepath on the left to Shore. As the track runs north look left to see the flat-topped ridge of East Hill **97**, with the village of Wardle at the foot of the scarp slope. Now follows a long, straight, level section. Bear left on reaching a wall, and follow it, keeping it on the left. By this point horse-riders – and certainly walkers – may be starting to find this part of the Loop a little unexciting. Be patient: the track turns left through a bridlegate in the wall, and suddenly fabulous views open up ahead over a range of deeply incised hills – Brow Hill, Wardle Hill, Middle Hill and Rough Hill – on the far side of the very beautiful Watergrove Valley. There's a wonderful feeling of space here.

Follow the track as it runs towards Watergrove Reservoir – with views over Rochdale beyond – with the Wardle Brook below right. The track passes through a gate by a deciduous plantation on the right and drops to the reservoir, passing the 'Life for a Life' memorial forest on the left **98**: a lovely plantation of (mainly) Scots pine, English oak, rowan and silver birch. Turn right **N** along the track by the reservoir to pass the car park and information centre on the left. (Turning left here will take you by bridleway back to the main Watergrove car park.)

Back at the information centre, take a break and spend a bit of time learning about the history of the valley – it's fascinating. (There are tethering rings for horses, and a water trough, up Ramsden Road; turn right at the end of the car park and these can be found a few yards up on the right **99**.) The 96-acre (39-hectare) reservoir holds 720 million gallons of water, and was constructed between August 1930 and April 1938 to supplement supplies to the increasing population of Rochdale; Watergrove village, plus a number of farms and houses, were lost beneath the waters in the process. An excellent map in the information centre gives details, and at times of low water the stone-setted way leading to Watergrove Mill can still be seen, just below the information centre. The ruins of several farms – many of which had been abandoned before the reservoir was built – are dotted around the valley, and there are one or two people alive today who can remember the valley at that time. In the late 1800s it supported a community of around 200 people involved in farming and small-scale local industry. Coal

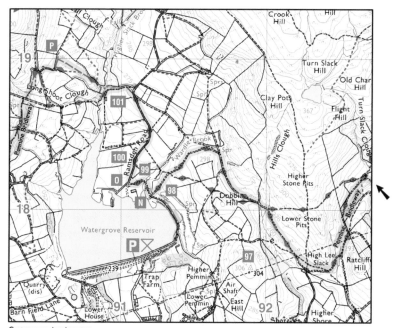

Contours are given in metres
The vertical interval is 5m

and gritstone were readily available (there are odd coal spoil heaps still visible); sheep grazed on the valley slopes; Higher Slack and Wardle Brooks supplied water. Quite apart from its value in terms of human history, Watergrove today is an important site for flora and fauna: skylark, curlew, common sandpiper, meadow pipit, wheatear and willow warbler may be seen, with wintering wildfowl species such as goldeneye, pochard and goosander. In the early 1990s an amazing 112 different species of flowers were listed in the valley – the information centre has a good supply of leaflets on what to look out for.

At the end of the car park turn right **O** up broad, stone-setted and walled Ramsden Road, which originally ran through Watergrove village. Pass the excavated ruins of the cottages at Little Town, and picnic area **100**, on the left. Go through a gate and follow the unwalled track, now gritty, across open moorland, passing the site of Steward Barn on the left. The track forks; take the left fork. Follow this track towards Middle Hill, passing through a bridlegate and then dropping downhill towards Higher Slack Brook, with Rotary Wood (oak and beech plantation) on the left **101**. There are two bridges over the brook (horses can drink here) – one open, one a railed bridlebridge.

The beautiful Watergrove Valley, an idyllically peaceful spot on a calm summer's day, yet home to around 200 people in the late 19th century.

Once over the brook, follow the right-hand path uphill to a field gate, and turn right. The path passes a pond below right in Higher Slack Clough, before turning sharp left in front of two twisted hawthorn trees. Follow the narrow, stone-setted path uphill between grass-covered slopes to a marker post in front of a broken wall.

Turn left **P**, keeping the wall on the right, with views of Rochdale and the reservoir ahead. Pass through a pair of gateposts and follow the wall, bearing right uphill. Pass through a clump of sycamore trees, and through another set of gateposts. Bear left – also on the Rochdale Way – and follow the track past the ruins of Middle Hill on the left. The track drops to cross the stream in Long Shoot Clough before levelling out – look left for distant views of the M62 viaduct, which comes as something of a surprise!

Bear right uphill and pass between stone posts, leaving the Watergrove Valley, a little regretfully, behind. The track keeps ahead by a large spoil heap on the right; drop left a little and continue straight ahead, on the lower path, with a leat (a small man-made water channel) alongside on the right. Where the path bears left downhill, turn right to cross the leat by a stone pillar; keep uphill to join a gritty track, and bear left. Keep along the level track – which has large pools of standing water after rainfall – until it splits; then take on the lower one (right), dropping to a fingerpost at a junction of tracks; the tower of St Bartholomew's Church 102 at Whitworth, erected 1874, is visible on the right.

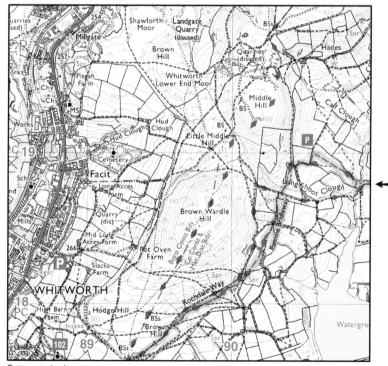

Contours are given in metres
The vertical interval is 5m

149

Turn left, and after 50 yards/metres turn right at the next fingerpost. Where the track leads into a tarmac lane ahead – and just beyond a tarmac lane leading off sharp left – turn left **Q** up a gritty track with a wooden post on the corner. Almost immediately the path bears right between wooden posts and a fence to pass the clubhouse of Lobden golf course across a green on the right. On reaching the car park, bear left along a gritty track; where that splits (the right fork leads to a house) bear left and follow the track along the lower edge of the golf course. Views of Spring Mill Reservoir **103** open up right. Pass along the lower slopes of Rushy Hill (1,034 feet/315 metres) on the left, and by Meadowmead Farm on the right. The track becomes rougher and drops downhill, with a wall on the right. Cross over an area of open pasture; the rutted path bears left, parallel to a wall on the right, with views to the church at Middle Healey **104** straight ahead. Cross a track leading to

Lonely sycamores, originally planted to provide shelter, mark the site of a long-abandoned farmstead at Watergrove. This species is particularly pollution resistant.

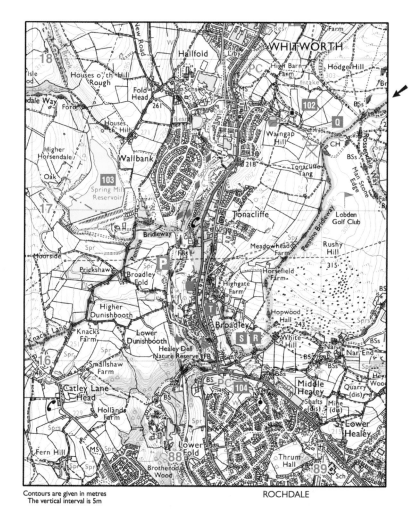

Contours are given in metres
The vertical interval is 5m

ROCHDALE

Hopwood Hall (left) and keep ahead on a gritty track, which bears right downhill to a marker post by a wall.

Turn right **R**, keeping the wall on the left. Pass through a metal gate and continue along the rough track, which drops downhill to pass a house above the track on the left. Where the track goes ahead under an arch, turn right **S** up a narrow, grassy path between high heather-covered banks. Where the path forks keep left, with a wall left. Pass a quarry pond on the right – up until about 1850 the moorland hereabouts was the source of stone setts that were used to pave the streets of Rochdale (birthplace of the Co-operative Movement in 1844) – and continue along the path to meet Highgate Lane **T** on the edge of Broadley.

The canals of the South Pennines

The industrial development of the South Pennines was aided by an overall improvement in communications. During the late 17th and 18th centuries, following the Turnpike Act of 1663, many packhorse trails were superseded by broader, better-surfaced turnpike roads. The next step was the construction of a great canal network, starting with the Rochdale Canal. Originally James Brindley, canal surveyor to the Duke of Bridgwater, was commissioned to oversee the project; by the time necessary funds had been raised he was dead, and John Rennie took over. This, the first canal to cross the Pennines, opened in 1804 and had a huge influence on the economic and industrial development of the area. Raw materials and finished products could more easily and economically be transported in bulk; the hamlet of Hebden Bridge, for example, rapidly transformed into a centre for the production of fustian, a thick cotton cloth. The canal ran for 33 miles (53 km) from the Bridgwater Canal in Manchester to Rochdale, continuing along the Calder Valley and onto Sowerby Bridge to link with the Calder and Hebble Navigation Canal. It was 15 feet (4.6 metres) wide – its vessels measured 14 feet

Bottomley Lock on the Rochdale Canal.

(4.3 metres) across – with 92 locks; several reservoirs, including Hollingworth Lake, were constructed to supply it. As the fortunes of local industry declined, so did those of the canal, and in 1841 the Manchester–Leeds Railway delivered another body blow. The last working barge travelled its length in 1937 and it closed in 1952. Fortunately, conservation groups have restored much of the canal for leisure activities, so preserving an important part of local industrial heritage.

The Huddersfield Narrow Canal was authorised in 1794. It did not open fully until 1811, on completion of the $3\frac{1}{4}$-mile (5.3-km) Standedge Tunnel – the longest and highest canal tunnel in the country – through the Pennine ridge. The canal runs for 20 miles (32.2 km) between Huddersfield and Ashton-under-Lyne. By 1900 it was virtually unused in the face of faster, cheaper rail transport; the last working boat used the tunnel in 1921. Thanks to enthusiasts, the canal was completely re-opened in 2001. Finally, the longest canal in Britain, the Leeds and Liverpool Canal, opened in 1816. This massive operation – the canal ran for 127 miles (204 km), had 91 locks and cost around £1 million – took 45 years to complete. Its last commercial use was in the early 1960s.

One immensely satisfying aspect of the Loop is that frequently you can look back on your ro

...e the wind farm top left, the bridleway below Stoodley Pike, and Salter Rake Gate bottom left.

155

PART THREE

USEFUL
INFORMATION

Transport

Traveline is a national number where you can be transferred to the area you are calling from or ask for information about areas you wish to travel to. This is therefore the most relevant number for all areas of the Pennine Bridleway and the Mary Towneley Loop: 0870 6082 608; www.traveline.org.uk

GMPTE (Greater Manchester Public Transport Executive): 0161 228 7811. www.gmpte.com

Derbyshire County Council Public Transport: www.derbybus.net

Public transport information: www.pti.org.uk

Public rail enquiries: 08457 484950 www.thetrainline.com

Trail services

Middleton Top to Littleborough

	km from trail	Link road	Rail stn	Bus	TIC	PO	Gen store	Toilets	Food & Drink	Accom
Matlock	7	A	•	•	•	•	•	•	•	•
Wirksworth	2	B	X	•	•	•	•	•	•	
Carsington	2	FP & Quiet	X	•	X	X	X	X	•	•
Grangemill/ Aldwark	2 3	FP B	X	X	X	X	X	X	•	•
Brassington	1	Quiet	X	•	X	X	X	X	•	X
Longcliffe	On	–	X	•	X	X	X	X	X	X
Pike Hall/ Gotham	On	–	X	•	X	X	X	X	X	•
Newhaven	1	A/B	X	•	X	X	X	X	•	•
Youlgreave	4	B/Q	X	•	X	•	•	•	•	•
Hartington	2 3	B Quiet	X	•	X	•	X	X	X	•
Monyash	3 2	Quiet B	X	•	X	•	•	•	•	•
Bakewell	10	B	X	•	•	•	•	•	•	•
Pomeroy	0.5	A	X	•	X	X	X	X	•	•
Chelmorton	0.5	–	X	•	X	X	X	X	•	•
Blackwell	0.5	Quiet	X	X	X	X	X	X	X	•
Taddington	2	B	X	•	X	X	X	X	•	•
Buxton	8	A	•	•	•	•	•	•	•	•

	km from trail	Link road	Rail stn	Bus	TIC	PO	Gen store	Toilets	Food & Drink	Accom
Wormhill	On	–	X	•	X	X	X	X	X	X
Peak Forest	On	–	X	•	X	•	•	X	•	•
Tideswell	1.5	FP	X	•	X	•	•	X	•	•
Hayfield	On	–	X	•	•	•	•	•	•	•
Chinley	3	Q	•	•	•	•	•	X	•	•
New Mills	2	BW	•	•	X	•	•	X	•	•
Birch Vale	On	–	X	•	X	•	•	X	•	•
Little Hayfield	1.5	Byway	X	•	X	X	X	X	•	•
Charlesworth	1	B	X	•	X	•	•	X	•	•
Simmondley	1	B	X	•	X	X	X	X	X	X
Glossop	2.5	B	•	•	•	•	•	•	•	•
Hadfield	On	–	•	•	•	•	•	•	•	•
(Broadbottom	On	–	•	•	•	•	•	•	•	X)
(Hollingworth	On	–	X	•	X	•	•	X	•	•)
Tintwistle	On	–	X	•	X	X	•	X	X	X
Stalybridge	3	B	•	•	•	•	•	•	•	•
Millbrook	1	Quiet	X	•	X	X	X	X	•	X
Carrbrook	0.5	–	X	•	X	X	X	X	•	X
Greenfield	On	–	•	•	X	•	•	•	•	•
Uppermill	On	–	X	•	•	•	•	•	•	•
Diggle	On	-	X	•	X	•	•	•	X	•
Delph	3	B	X	•	X	X	•	X	•	•
Dobcross	1	B	X	•	X	•	•	X	•	•
Marsden	3.5	BW	X	•	•	•	•	•	•	•
Denshaw	1.5	A	X	•	X	X	X	X	X	X
Smithy Bridge/ Hollingworth	1	B	•	•	X	•	•	•	•	•
Littleborough	2	B	•	•	•	•	•	•	•	•

Mary Towneley Loop

	km from trail	Link road	Rail stn	Bus	TIC	PO	Gen store	Toilets	Food & Drink	Accom
Summit	On	–	X	•	X	•	•	X	•	X
Shore	1	Quiet	X	•	X	X	X	X	•	X
Wardle	1.5	Quiet	X	•	X	•	•	X	•	•
Whitworth	1.5	A	X	•	X	•	•	•	•	•
Catley Ln Head	0.5	Quiet	X	•	X	X	X	X	•	•
Waterfoot	On	–	X	•	X	•	•	•	•	•
Edgeside	On	–	X	•	X	X	•	X	•	X
Lumb	On	–	X	•	X	X	X	X	•	•
Water	0.5	BW	X	•	X	X	•	X	•	X

Key: A = A road, B = B road, BW = bridleway, FP = footpath, Q = quiet, • = yes, X = no

	km from trail	Link road	Rail stn	Bus	TIC	PO	Gen store	Toilets	Food & Drink	Accom
Holme Chapel	On	–	X	•	X	X	•	X	•	•
Worsthorne	2	BW	X	•	X	•	•	X	•	X
Colden / Blackshaw Head	0.5	Quiet	X	•	X	•	•	X	•	•
Heptonstall	2.5	Quiet	X	•	X	•	•	X	•	•
Hebden Bridge	3	Quiet	•	•	•	•	•	•	•	•
Todmorden	1.5	Quiet	•	•	•	•	•	•	•	•
Mankinholes	On	–	X	•	X	X	X	X	•	•
Walsden	0.5	Quiet	•	•	X	X	•	X	•	•
Calderbrook	0.5	Quiet	X	X	X	X	X	X	•	X
Bacup	3	A	X	•	X	•	•	X	•	•

Cycle hire

Derbyshire to the Mary Towneley Loop

Carsington Water Sports & Cycle Hire, Carsington, Derbyshire DE6 1PZ. Tel. 01629 540478.

Middleton Top Visitor & Cycle Hire Centre, High Peak Trail, Wirksworth, Derbyshire DE4 4L. Tel. 01629 823204.

Ashbourne Cycle Hire Centre, Mapleton Lane, Ashbourne, Derbyshire DE6 2AA. Tel. 01335 343156.

Parsley Hay Cycle Hire, High Peak Trail, Nr Buxton, Derbyshire SK17 0DG. Tel. 01298 84493.

Hayfield Information & Cycle Hire Centre, Sett Valley Trail, Hayfield, Derbyshire SK22 2ES. Tel. 01663 746222.

Chris Paulson Cycles, 246 Yorkshire Street, Rochdale, Lancashire OL16 2DP. Tel. 01706 633426.

Blazing Saddles, 23 Market Street, Hebden Bridge, W. Yorkshire HX7 6EU. Tel. 01422 844435.

Cycle shops

Derbyshire to the Mary Towneley Loop

Fearn Stanley & Son, 19 Bakewell Road, Matlock, Derbyshire. Tel. 01629 582089.

Terry's Cycle Emporium, Peak House, St John's Street, Wirksworth, Derbyshire. Tel. 01629 826747.

Buxton Bikes, 2a Dale Road, Buxton, Derbyshire. Tel. 01298 79880.

Mark Anthony Cycles, 115 Spring Gardens, Buxton, Derbyshire. Tel. 01298 72114.

Sett Valley Cycles, 9 Union Road, New Mills, Derbyshire. Tel. 01663 742629.

The Bike Factory, Vernon House, Beach Road, Whaley Bridge, Derbyshire. Tel. 01663 735020.

High Peak Cycles, 93–93 High Street West, Glossop, Derbyshire. Tel. 01457 861535.

K G Bikes, 18 North Street, Glossop, Derbyshire. Tel. 01457 862427.

Bike Lane, 180 Old Street, Ashton-u-Lyne, Tameside OL6. Tel. 0161 339 3777.

TPS Cycles, 98 Penny Meadow, Ashton-u-Lyne, Tameside. Tel. 0161 339 4236.

Mossley Cycles, 12 Manchester Road, Mossley, Tameside. Tel. 01457 835913.

SD Cycles, 384 Huddersfield Road, Millbrook, Stalybridge, Tameside SK15 3ET. Tel. 0161 3387598.

Bridge Cycles, 85 Market Street, Stalybridge, Tameside SK15. Tel. 0161 3387644.

B H D Cycles, 149 Aston Road, Oldham OL8. Tel. 0161 620 4319.

Oldham Cycle Centre, 87 Lees Road, Oldham OL4. Tel. 0161 624 8260.

Skidmores Cycles, 37 Union Street, Oldham OL1. Tel. 0161 624 5912.

Suntal Cycles, 45–47 Ripponden Road, Oldham OL1. Tel. 0161 624 7409.

Burnley Cycle Centre, 30–34 Briercliffe Road, Burnley, Lancashire. Tel. 01282 433981.

Queengate Cycles, 328 Colne Road, Burnley, Lancashire BB10 1ED. Tel. 01282 709937.

On Yer Bike, Queen Street, Burnley, Lancashire. Tel. 01282 438855

Ride On, 213–15 Bacup Road, Rawtenstall, Lancashire BB4 7PA. Tel. 01706 831101.

Kingsway Sports, 240 Oldham Road, Rochdale, Lancashire. Tel. 01706 646686.

Chris Paulson Cycles, 246 Yorkshire Street, Rochdale, Lancashire OL16 2DP. Tel. 01706 633426.

The Bike Shop, 55–61 Market Street, Whitworth, Lancashire OL12 8RW. Tel. 01706 657162.

Blazing Saddles, 23 Market Street, Hebden Bridge, W. Yorkshire HX7 6EU. Tel. 01422 844435.

DC Mansfield, 9 New Road, Mytholmroyd, W. Yorkshire OL12 5DZ. Tel. 01422 884397.

Harry Ingham, 120 Rochdale Road, Todmorden, W. Yorkshire OL14 7NA. Tel. 01706 812148.

Vale Cycles, 48 Burnley Road, Todmorden, W. Yorkshire. Tel. 01706 816558.

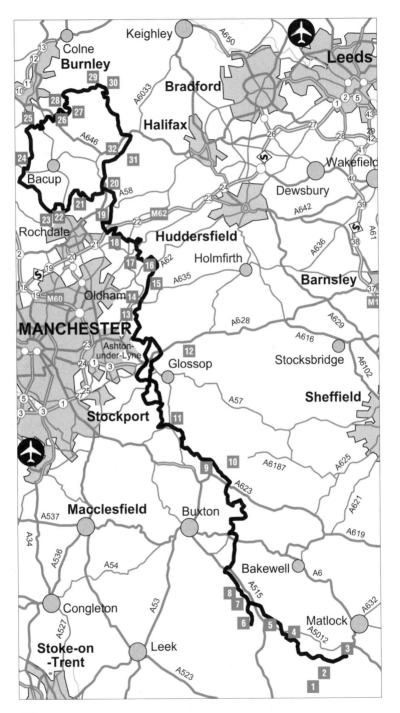

Car Parks and Trail Facilities

Derbyshire to the Mary Towneley Loop

	Car park location	km from trail	Link road	TIC	Toilets	Disabled facilities	Suitable for H boxes	Other facilities (see key)	Car park charge
1	Carsington Wtr	3	Quiet	•	•	•	Cars only	–	•
2	Carsington–Sheepwash cp	2	FP	X	X	X	Yes	DW, BH, C	X
3	Middleton Top	On	–	•	•	•	Ltd use	BH, W	•
4	Minninglow	On	–	X	X	X	Cars only	–	X
5	Friden	On	–	X	X	X	Cars only	–	X
6	Hartington	On	–	•	•	•	Yes	T, P, S, K, R, W, HR	•
7	Parsley Hay	On	–	•	•	•	Cars only	BH, K, W	•
8	Sparklow	On	–	X	X	X	Cars only	–	X
9	Rushup Edge	On	–	X	X	X	Cars only	*	X
10	Mam Tor	3	BW	X	X	X	Ltd use	–	X
11	Hayfield	On	–	•	•	•	Yes	R, W, BH	•
12	Torside (Longdendale)	5	BW	X	•	•	Yes	HR, RV	X
13	Carrbrook	On	–	X	X	X	Yes (small)	–	X
14	Friezland	On	–	X	X	•	Yes	R, T, HR	X
15	Diggle	On	–	X	X	X	Cars only	–	X
16	Brun Clough (Standedge A62)	On	BW	X	X	X	Yes	–	X
17	Castleshaw	On	Quiet	X	X	X	Yes	–	X
18	Ogden	On	BW	X	•	X	Cars only	–	X
19	Hollingworth Lk	On	–	•	•	•	Yes	DW, C, T	•
20	Summit	On	–	–	–	–	Small	–	X
21	Watergrove	0.5	–	•	•	•	Yes	R, T, HR	X
22	Healey Dell	0.5	–	X	X	X	Ltd use	Layby	X
23	Catley Ln Hd	On	–	X	X	X	Ltd use	Layby	X
24	Waterfoot	On	–	X	X	X	Cars only	–	X
25	Clowbridge	2	BW	X	•	•	Yes	R, HR	X
26	Deerplay Moor	On	–	X	X	X	Ltd use	–	X
27	Long Causeway	0.5	B	X	X	X	Yes	–	X
28	Hurstwood	1	B	X	X	X	Yes	–	X
29	Widdop	On	–	X	X	X	Ltd use	–	X
30	Clough Foot	On	–	X	X	X	Ltd use	–	X
31	Withens Clough	3	BW	X	X	X	Ltd use	–	X
32	Salter Rake	On	–	X	X	X	Ltd use	–	X

BH = Bike hire, C = cafe, DW = Drinking water, HR = Hitching rail, K = Kiosk,
P = Paddock, R = Ramp, RV = Refreshment van, S = Horse shelter, T = Drinking trough,
W = Water, * = Layby large enough for box or trailer for emergency pick-up

Tourist Information Centres

Matlock Tourist Information Centre, Crown Square, Matlock,
    Derbyshire DE4 3AT. Tel. 01629 583388.
Ashbourne Tourist Information, 13 Market Place, Ashbourne,
    Derbyshire DE6 1EU. Tel. 01335 343666.
Bakewell Tourist Information, Old Market Hall, Bridge Street,
    Bakewell, Derbyshire DE45 1DS. Tel. 01629 813227.
Buxton Tourist Information, The Crescent, Buxton, Derbyshire
    SK17 6BQ. Tel. 01298 25106.
Glossop Tourist Information, The Gatehouse, Victoria Street,
    Glossop, Derbyshire SK13 8HT. Tel. 01457 855920.
Tameside Tourist Information, Tameside Council Offices,
    Wellington Road, Ashton-u-Lyne OL6 6DL. Tel. 0161 343 4343.
Holmfirth Tourist Information, 49–51 Hudderfield Road,
    Holmfirth, W. Yorkshire HD9 3JP. Tel. 01484 222444.
Saddleworth Tourist Information, Saddleworth Museum,
    High Street, Uppermill, Oldham OL3 6HS. Tel. 01457 870336.
Oldham Tourist Information, 12 Albion Street, Oldham
    OL1 3BD. Tel. 0161 627 1024.
Rochdale Tourist Information Centre, The Clock Tower, Town
    Hall, Rochdale OL16 1AB. Tel. 01706 864928.
Rossendale Tourist Information Centre, 41–45 Kay Street,
    Rawtenstall, Rossendale, Lancashire BB4 7LS.
    Tel. 01706 844678.
Burnley Tourist Information, The Bus Station, Croft Street, Burnley
    BB1 5AX. Tel. 01282 664421. E-mail: tic@burnley.gov.uk
Hebden Bridge & Canal Visitor Centre, New Road, Hebden
    Bridge, W. Yorkshire HX7 8AD. Tel. 01422 843831.
Todmorden Tourist Information, 15 Burnley Road, Todmorden,
    W. Yorkshire. Tel. 01706 818181.

Saddlers

Matlock Saddlery, 85–87 Wellington Street, Matlock,
    Derbyshire. Tel. 01629 583185.
Peak Dale Saddlery, Hallsteads Close, Dove Holes, Buxton,
    Derbyshire SK17 8BC. Tel. 01298 814040.
Country Sport, 31 Station Road, Hadfield, Glossop, Derbyshire.
    Tel. 01457 867643.
Hound, Horse & Rider, 75–79 King Street, Dunkinfield,
    Tameside SK16 4NQ. Tel. 0161 330 5798.
Bridge Saddlery, 30a Dale Street, Milnrow, Rochdale.
    Tel. 01706 645146.

Naylors Saddlery Stores, 472 Edenfield Road, Rochdale.
Tel. 01706 631909.
Victorian Saddles, 115 Halifax Road, Rochdale.
Tel. 01706 644490.
M. Miller, 624 Burnley Road East, Whitewill Bottom,
Rossendale, Lancashire BB4 9NT. Tel. 01706 226983.
Moody Mares, Briar Hey, Mytholmroyd, Hebden Bridge,
W. Yorkshire. Tel. 01422 886060.
Suzie Vanderpeer, The Saddlery Workshop, Higher Stoodley
Cottage, Lee Bottom Road, Todmorden, W. Yorkshire
OL14 6HD. Tel. 01706 812488.

Farriers

Peter King, Bent Farm, Farley, Matlock, Derbyshire DE4 5LT.
Tel. 01629 582792.
Michael Bate, Cliff Cottage, 41 Main Road, Whatstandwell,
Matlock, Derbyshire DE4 5HE. Tel. 01773 856014.
Mobile: 07980 211964.
Darren Ainsworth, The Georgian Forge, Blackwell Hall Farm,
Blackwell, Derbyshire. Mobile: 07770 777708.
M. Caley, 9 Sunnyfields, Brier Tor-Bar Road, Buxton,
Derbyshire SK17 9PT. Tel. 01298 27483.
Phillip Jordan, 463 Bury Old Road, Prestwich, Manchester
M25 1WJ. Tel. 0161 798 7831.
P. Travis, 41b Dobcross New Road, Dobcross, Oldham OL3 5AY.
Tel. 01457 874525.
Derek Addy, 183 Rooley Moor Road, Rochdale OL12 7DQ. Tel.
01706 647969.
Sam Sagar, The Homestead, Carlton Street, Todmorden Road,
Bacup, Lancashire OL13 9DT. Tel. 07974 155645.
P. K. Lamb, 14 Bankfield Terrace, Stacksteads, Bacup,
Lancashire. Tel. 01706 878671.
Colin Thompson, Knowsley Farm, Shawforth, Whitworth,
Lancashire OL12 8XE. Tel. 01706 853884. Mobile: 07977 883375.
Alec Thorpe, Eagley Bank, Whitworth, Lancashire OL12 8XE.
Tel. 01706 852730. Mobile: 07973 443116.
Raymond Kay, Lancashire. Tel. 01254 813095.
B. Thorne, W. Yorkshire. Tel. 01422 372279.

Please note that it can be difficult to obtain the services of a
farrier at short notice and it is recommended that long-distance
riders carry a protective equiboot for their horse in case of
emergencies.

Vets

S. C. Reeve, 113 Church Street, Matlock, Derbyshire DE45 3BZ. Tel. 01629 582844.

McMurtry & Harding, 34 Market Place, Ashbourne, Derbyshire DE6 1ES. Tel. 01335 342227.

Francis & Herdman, Milford Farm, Mill Street, Bakewell, Derbyshire DE45 1DX. Tel. 01629 812640.

Overdale Veterinary Centre, New Market Street, Buxton, Derbyshire SK17 6LP. Tel. 01298 23499.

Grove Veterinary Hospital, 1&2 Hibbert Street, New Mills, Derbyshire SL2 3JJ. Tel. 01663 745294.

J. N. MacDonald, Sylvan House, Sylvan Street, Maine Road, Oldham, Lancashire OL9 6LX. Tel. 0161 624 7102.

Mearley Veterinary Group, Mearley Veterinary Centre, Holden Street, Clitheroe, Lancashire BB7 1LU. Tel. 01200 423763.

Stanley House Veterinary Surgeons, 20 Albert Road, Colne, Lancashire BB8 OAA. Tel. 01282 563892.

Holborow & Tapsfield-Wright, 41 Burnley Road, Todmorden, Lancashire OL14 7BU. Tel. 01706 814770.

Sage Veterinary Group, Netherfield House, Salisbury Road, Bradford, W. Yorkshire BD12 OAA. Tel. 01274 679192.

Aireworth Vet Centre, Airworth Road, Keighley, W. Yorkshire BD214DJ. Tel. 01535 602988.

Ashfield Veterinary Group, Oakroyd Veterinary Surgery, 213 High Street, Wibsey, Bradford, W. Yorkshire BD6 1JU. Tel. 01274 691318.

Hind & Partners, 10 Blackwall, Halifax, W. Yorkshire HX1 2BE. Tel. 01422 354106.

Horse Transport

Mr Spencer, UK Horse Transport, Wood Cottage, Alkrington, Middleton, Manchester M24 1WE. Tel. 0161 654 8278

Mike Tilsley, Hargate Hill Equestrian Centre, , Charlesworth, Glossop, Derbyshire. Tel. 01457 865518, Mobile: 07860 927059

Robert Leak, Hawkshaw Horse Transport, Hawkshaw Lane, Hawkshaw, Bury, Lancashire BL8 4LB. Tel. 01204 882708, Mobile: 07855 958380, hawkshawhorsetransport.co.uk

Boothroyden Horse Transport, Bothroyden Cottages, Boothroyden Terrace, Higher Blackley, Manchester M9 OSB. Tel. 0161 653 6483

Roy, R&R Horse Transport, Manor House Farm, 4 Manor Road, Clayton West, Huddersfield HD8 9QD. Tel. 01484 866620, Mobile: 07977 272823

Bibliography

Alderson, Caroline, *Touring and Exploring the South Pennines* (CP Printing and Publishing Ltd).

Barnes, Bernard, *A Passage through Time: Saddleworth Roads and Trackways* (Saddleworth Historical Society, 1981).

Brooks, John, *Derbyshire Car Tours* (Ordnance Survey and Jarrold Publishing, 1996).

Goldthorpe, Ian, *Further Rossendale Rambles* (Rossendale Groundwork Trust, 1991).

Hopkins, Tony, *National Trail Guide: Pennine Way South* (Aurum Press, 2002).

Hopkins, Tony, *The Peak District* (AA Publishing, 2003).

Mee, Arthur (ed.), *The King's England – Derbyshire and The Peak* (Hodder and Stoughton, 1949).

Peak District Map and Guidebook (Goldeneye).

Powell, Joyce, *Longdendale Introspect*.

Pridmore, Elizabeth Jane, *Fabric of the Hills* (The Standing Conference of South Pennine Authorities, 1989).

Quayle, Tom, *Reservoirs in the Hills* (Longdendale Amenity Society, 1977).

Rickwood, Dr Pat, *The Story of Access in the Peak District* (Peak National Park, 1982).

Rodgers, Frank, *Curiosities of Derbyshire and the Peak District* (Derbyshire Countryside Ltd, 2000).

Sellers, Gladys, *Walking in the South Pennines* (Cicerone Press, 1991).

Smith, Roly, *Peak District* (Insight Compact Guide, 1997).

Smith, Roly, *The Official National Park Guide: The Peak District* (Pevensey Press, 2000).

Sparks, Jon, *50 Walks in Lancashire and Cheshire* (AA Publishing, 2003).

Spray, Martin, *Peak District Place Names* (J. N. M. Publications, 1989).

Taylor, Hugh, and McCrossan, Moira, *The Hidden Places of Derbyshire, including the Peak District* (Travel Publishing Ltd, 2002).

The Changing Face of Rossendale (four titles) (Rossendale Borough Council and Rossendale Groundwork Trust).

The Walker's Map and Guide to Calderdale's Far North-West (Countryside Commission).

Thornber, Titus, *Seen on the Packhorse Trails* (South Pennine Packhorse Trails Trust, 2002).

Thorold, Henry, *Derbyshire: A Shell Guide* (Faber & Faber, 1972).

It is impossible to list all the material consulted while preparing this book; the above represents the main sources of reference.

Ordnance Survey maps covering the Pennine Bridleway

Derbyshire to the South Pennines

Explorer Outdoor Leisure 1:25 000: 24 The Peak District –
White Peak Area; 1 The Peak District – Dark Peak Area;
21 South Pennines

Useful Addresses

Pennine Bridleway Team, Countryside Agency, 7th Floor
Bridgewater House, Whitworth Street, Manchester M1 6LT.
Tel. 0161 237 1061.
E-mail: julie.thompson@countryside.gov.uk (for route and
development);
wendy.wilson@countryside.gov.uk (for general information)
Website: www.countryside.gov.uk

Pennine Way National Trail, National Trail Officer, The
Countryside Agency, 4th Floor Victoria Wharf, No 4 The
Embankment, Sovereign Street, Leeds LS1 4BA.
Tel: 0113 246 9222. E-mail: pennineway@countryside.gov.uk
Website: www.nationaltrail.co.uk

Pennine Cycleway, Information Department, Sustrans, Crown
House, 37–41 Prince Street, Bristol BS1 4PF.
Tel: 0845 113 0065. E-mail: info@sustrans.org.uk
Website: www.penninecycleway-north.co.uk;
www.sustrans.org.uk

Trans Pennine Trail, c/o Barnsley MBC, Kendray Street,
Barnsley S70 2TN. Tel: 01226 772574.
E-mail: transpenninetrail@barnsley.gov.uk
Website: www.transpenninetrail.org.uk

British Horse Society, Stoneleigh Deer Park, Kenilworth,
Warwickshire CV8 2XZ. Tel. 01926 707700.

CTC Off Road, Mick Ives, 77 Mill Hill, Baginton, Coventry
CV8 3AG. Tel. 02476 303924.

Ordnance Survey, Romsey Road, Maybush, Southampton
SO16 4GU. Tel. 08456 050505. Website: www.ordsvy.gov.uk

Youth Hostels Association, Trevelyan House, Dimple Road,
Matlock, Derbyshire DE4 3YH. Tel. 0870 870 8808.
Website: www.yha.org.uk